Herit
in New

Locations of Walks

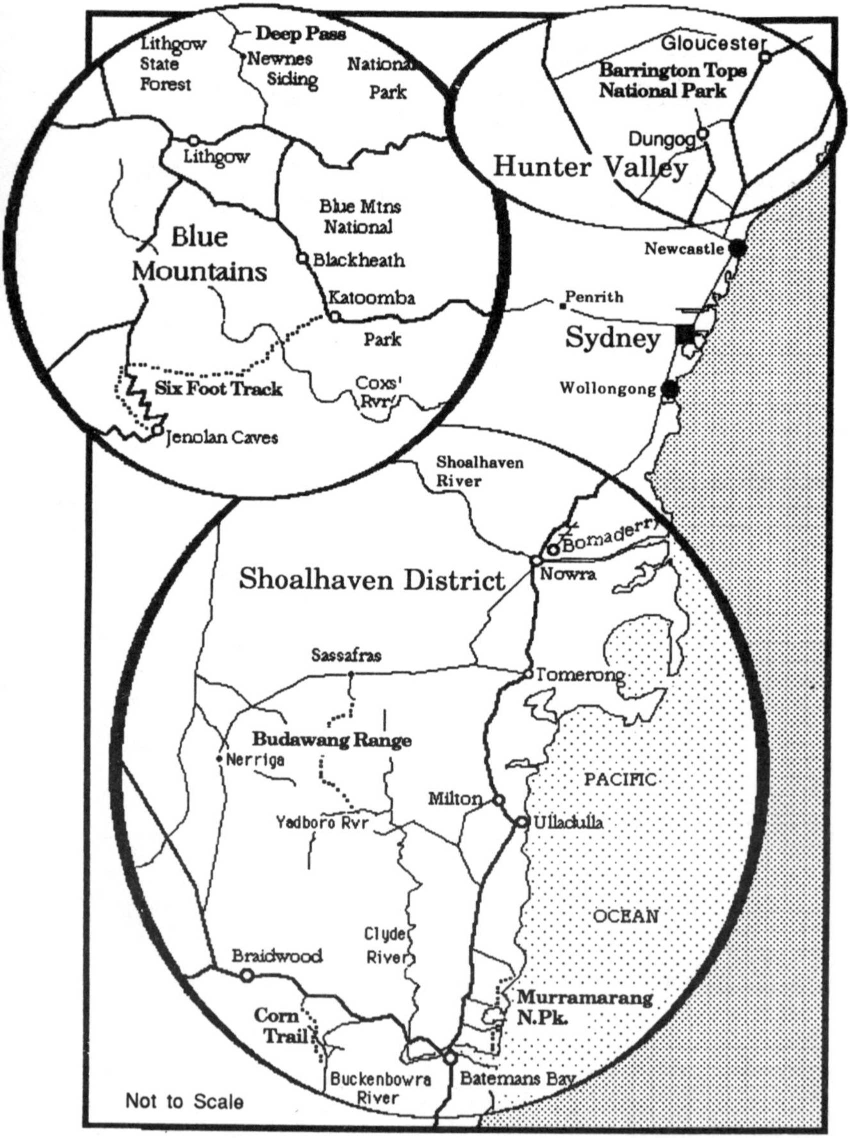

Heritage Walks in New South Wales

Garry McDougall

Kangaroo Press

for

Anna and Virginia

First published in 1992 by Kangaroo Press Pty Ltd
3 Whitehall Road (P.O. Box 75) Kenthurst NSW 2156
Typeset by J.C. Type, Sydney
Printed by The Book Printer, Maryborough, Victoria

ISBN 0 86417 383 0

Contents

Map Key

- Vehicle access
- Caravan Park
- 4WD access
- Crash site
- Trig point
- Point of Interest
- Township
- Hill
- Locked gate
- Trig Point
- Abor. Paintings
- Route without Track
- Route with Track
- Road: public/forest
- Ocean, lake
- Rock shelves
- Urban area
- Swamp/Peat bog
- Creek/River
- Cliffs
- Camp Site

Acknowledgments

Many people have contributed to this work, and I'd like to thank each of the following: Ricci Simpson and Allen Thomas have provided comment, criticisms, maps and photographs on the Corn Trail. Allen's map is found inside, and Ricci's botanical study of the trail has proven a useful and comprehensive work. Joan Childs spent considerable time reading and commenting on the text, and saved me from exasperation at my own shortcomings. Barbara offered very welcome advice on written expression. Her warmth and welcome in Leura has been a great comfort. Mick Childs and John Walker, fellow guides, have been helpful in providing extra information and experience. The staff of the National Parks and Wildlife Service's Raymond Terrace office (especially Chris Howard), have been most helpful. The NSW Dept of Conservation and Land Management (especially Wilf Hilder and Rick Noble), has provided information and support whenever it was needed. They produce some excellent brochures on their Six Foot Track and other walks. Many give good historical background notes. I also acknowledge Jim Smith and Wilf Hilder's worthy work on the Six Foot Track. It has greatly increased our knowledge of the walking tradition in the Blue Mountains. Lastly I thank Virginia and Anna for their companionship, support and forbearance. I've met many others on the tracks, exchanging ideas and information which have enhanced my knowledge. These people go unnamed, but not unthanked.

Introduction

Terra Australis incognita, the unknown southern continent. The Greeks, Arabs, Chinese and Indians all had ideas about where it was and what was there, but none visited it. Only in the 18th century did a few small European nations, particularly Britain, discover its natural and scientific wonders. James Cook's three year journey to record the transit of Venus across the sun returned home with 1000 new species of plants, 500 fish, 500 skins of animals, innumerable insects, rocks and native artefacts and the vocabularies of unheard of languages, much of it bounty from Australia. It was Europe's first sampling of Australia's natural heritage.

Later, armed with a convenient notion of a land empty of civilised people, the English occupied the continent. In the standard diction of economists the land was a 'given' resource, there to be cultivated as they saw fit. Farming, settlement, mining and other industry proceeded at a furious pace; from 1788, what was 'given' was now taken for wealth creation.

Eventually the European occupants came to regret some of their actions: land became overstocked; forestry exploitation was chaotic and rapacious; in Sydney and Melbourne, expansion was unchecked and land clearance was guided largely by greed and ignorance. Many began to ask what could be done to preserve the Great South Land's rivers, land plants, animals and birdlife.

In New South Wales, early attempts at conservation were rather feeble: early colonial tree preservation orders, the (much later) banning of koala shooting and, from the 1870s, greater management and control of forest exploitation. As controlling measures they aimed to reduce future problems or preserve resources for future exploitation; not to conserve our natural heritage.

In 1879 regret perhaps became resolution—and action—for the first time with the creation of The National Park ('Royal' was only added in 1955). For the first time land was permanently set aside for general recreational use.

At first, the national park concept was primitive. It was based on the English parkland model, and the deer park on the nearby river foreshores was considered an enhancement. More deer were added in 1885 and 1893. Before 1922, the controlling Trust raised funds by allowing selective logging.

The national park concept has since been considerably refined. In 1967 NSW introduced Australia's first National Parks and Wildlife Bill, introducing a secure, professionally managed national parks and nature conservation system.

In 1970 a national park was defined as:

> a relatively large area set aside for its features of predominantly unspoiled natural landscape, flora and fauna, permanently dedicated for public enjoyment, education and inspiration, and protected from all interference other then essential management practices, so that its natural attributes are protected.

Four of the following six essays cover walks within national parks. Of these, three cover all or large sections of Murramarang, Budawang and Barrington Tops National Parks. The Deep Pass walk is in a small section of Wollemi National Park. Other walks are under the authority of the Forestry Commission (Corn Trail) and the dept of Conservation and Land Management (Six Foot Track). Although not the custodian of all natural heritage, it is national park status that affords the best protection.

Use of the word 'heritage' is usually associated with 'bricks and mortar', the preservation of buildings, constructions and ruins. These are reminders or icons of the past; they have elements of design and style, and they also have an 'aura'. They are gateways to the past.

On most of the walks in this book there is some 'bricks and mortar' heritage, if only on a small scale. Barrington Tops, for example, has forestry and settlement ruins dating from the late 19th century; the Six Foot Track has the ruins of an abandoned mining town and convict graves; Deep Pass has Aboriginal carvings of unknown age, and Murramarang has an Aboriginal mine site over 600 years old.

Significantly, many tracks are part of a wider concept of heritage. The Corn Trail, for example, is a heritage item in itself as it is part of the 1830s track that first linked Braidwood to the coast. The Six Foot Track is a reminder of Australia's first brush with Romanticism.

Natural and cultural heritage are often entwined in this way.

Development often impinges on unspoilt areas, so that what has heritage value is not always clear. International conventions and legal status add new dimensions. The themes and issues of nature conservation can be working tools for clarifying aspects of heritage.

All of the walks in this collection have heritage value; whether the 'natural' heritage of unspoiled wilderness that we hope will be preserved for future generations, or 'cultural' heritage—reminders of Australia's past (both Aboriginal and white), or both.

Chapter 1, Romancing the Six Foot Track, reviews the history of the Track (and the history of bushwalking in Australia), investigates its romantic associations, and poses the question: is the popularity of the Six Foot Track today a sign of a modern form of Romanticism?

The Corn Trail, in Buckenbowra State Forest, is another interesting track. Chapter 2 is an attempt to record the joys of the experience, from visual and other sensual delights to the entertainment gained from observation and curiosity.

In the Budawang Range walk (the only walk in the book that goes through true wilderness), the role of bushwalkers has been significant in shaping the area's nomenclature, use and management to a degree rarely surpassed anywhere else in Australia. All who have walked the range hold it dear to their hearts. Budawang magic is mysterious, at least to me, and the account in chapter 3 gives a taste of that magic, particularly in Monolith Valley.

Murramarang National Park's proximity to settlement prompts a number of thoughts on coastal development. It is the only coastal park examined. In the light of recent events the thought of excessive coastal development, of bribery and corruption and, worse of all, coping with the result, is horrifying. For Murramarang, set between the populations of Canberra, Wollongong and Sydney, the despoliation of the coastal environment has already begun. What is being done? What is there that is so valuable? The 14 walks cover past Aboriginal habitation and culture, geological past, botanical curiosities, and future development along the park's edges.

The Barrington Tops region includes both national park and state forest. Little has been written about the area, so here is the most detailed (non-scientific) account yet, plus a look at Aboriginal habitation of rainforest areas.

Deep Pass is part of the much neglected Wollemi National Park. This essay is a reflection on the nature of 'conservation' and management. It's only a short walk to the deep chasms of the Pass, a wonderful introduction to place as paradise.

Practical Information

If this book inspires you to put on your walking boots, some 53 walks are covered in the book (for the full list see p.13). You'll find information on:

- location and access routes
- maps for most walks, some providing previously unpublished details
- seasonal information
- descriptions of walks, particularly for Murramarang and Barrington Tops National Parks
- where to find further information, including maps and further reading

The Walking Tradition

These walks are heritage walks, not only because some played a role in the opening up of NSW, but also because they are part of the walking tradition developed mainly by British and German immigrants. Walking in Europe became popular in the mid- to late-19th century. For the middle classes there was no better way of gaining a sense of fitness and well being.

Walking was particularly popular amongst literary and artistic types, who found romance in Nature, and escape from the more harrowing aspects of modern industrial capitalism. Perhaps this explains why early written accounts emphasised the romantic side of walking: the landscapes, and the writer's response to his surroundings.

In NSW the figure of John Le Gay Brereton, journalist and (in later life) Professor of English at Sydney University, is important. He wrote *Landlopers* in 1896, an account of a long walk, noted by poet and friend R.D. Fitzgerald as 'an early and very gentle Australian picaresque; it deserves to be known as an Australian masterpiece'.

Compatriot H. Tompkins then wrote *With Swag and Billy* in 1907, arguably Australia's first recreational walking book. It lacked Brereton's fine style, but at least gave full consideration to sensibilities as much as to the carrying of billies.

Since those days the literary standard of recreational walking books has sadly declined. The result is that values, issues and ideas have been either bluntly asserted or completely ignored. Writers seem to be suspicious of, or lack confidence in, pursuing them, limiting themselves to giving sterile directions.

Today, bushwalkers and nature conservationists are amongst the most passionate and sensitive people one might happily meet. Unease about the use of language—and about the use of recreational walking books—is decreasing. Yet many in the walking fraternity still ask: don't these books just bring more people to national parks? Doesn't this just ensure more damage, more rubbish and more abuse of our unspoilt areas?

These are legitimate concerns, and, thank goodness, there are reasonable answers. Firstly, where there is national park status there is management. As imperfect as it this may be, the staff of the National Parks and Wildlife Service (NPWS) are dedicated people striving to preserve the natural ecology of the areas under their care. It is their role (and ours) to see that destructive elements are kept from damaging our heritage.

Secondly, no-one is born with conservation values, nor are such values all that meaningful when held in abstract. They are best acquired by knowledge and experience, by enjoying walks in national parks, state forests and elsewhere. Books are one gateway to those experiences.

All of us have a role in effective guardianship, and in introducing others to the bush. Those of us who love national parks, walking tracks and wilderness areas can't advance conservation values while they are selfishly guarding them from others.

So this book aims to offer greater opportunities for walking in NSW, a broader notion of our heritage, and an opportunity to join the walking tradition.

Walking is the great collection of joys, challenges and social rewards.The possibilities for walking in this state alone are greater than the recreational resources of most nations. I encourage you to visit, enjoy, be curious, and make appropriate use of NSW walking tracks and national parks. In the meantime enjoy the pleasure of reading.

Garry McDougall

List of Suggested Walks

Romancing the Six Foot Track

1. Katoomba to Jenolan Caves
2. Megalong Valley to Coxs River
3. Nellies Glen
4. Jenolan State Forest to Katoomba
5. Kiaora Hill

The Corn Trail

6. The Corn Trail
7. The Buckenbowra River

Murramarang National Park

Northern

8. Murramarang Point
9. Snapper Point
10. Pretty Beach to Durras Mtn
11. Durras Mtn, Clear Pt, Pretty Beach
12. Pebbly Beach surrounds

Central

13. Pebbly to Clear Point
14. Pebbly to Depot Beach
15. Depot Beach to Nth Durras
16. Nth to Sth Durras

Southern

17. North Head
18. Richmond Beach to North Head
19. Sth Durras to Richmond Beach

Budawang Magic

20. Newhaven Gap to Yadboro River
21. Hidden Valley
22. Yadboro to Monolith Valley
23. Yadboro to The Castle/Cooyoyo
24. Wog Wog to Monolith Valley via Corang Peak

World Heritage Barrington Tops

Southern Slopes

25. Rocky Crosssing Track
26. Chicester State Forest
27. Jerusalem Creek track
28. Burraga Swamp
29. Cabre Bald
30. Gillwinga Track
31. Careys Peak via the Corker

Gloucester Tops

32. Laurie Lookout
33. Gloucester Falls Walk
34. Beech Forest Walk
35. Gloucester Tops Curcuit
36. The Link Track

Gloucester River Camping Area

37. Gloucester River Waterlife stroll

38. Sharpes Creek Track
39. Gloucester Upriver Walk
40. A Day Stroll
41. A Night Stroll

Barrington Tops

42. Beean Beean to Big Hole
43. Big Hole to Careys Peak
44. Junction Pools to Careys Peak
45. Careys Peak to Junction Pools curcuit
46. Junction Pools to Beean Beean Plain
47. Wombat Creek and Selby Alley Hut

Polblue Access Tracks

48. Polblue to Little Murrays
49. Little Murrays to Beean Beean Plain

Major Treks

50. Polblue to Gloucester Tops
51. Barrington House to the Tops via The Corker
52. Polblue to Dungog via Gloucester Tops

Deep Pass

53. Local tracks in Deep Pass

Romancing the Six Foot Track

When it comes to heritage walks the Six Foot Track has an unparalleled place in Australia's walking history. Built in the 1880s the Track starts at Katoomba, capital of the Blue Mountains, and concludes at Jenolan Caves. In between it is swallowed by grand Blue Mountains countryside: rounded or steep hills, open woodland, forests of dappled light, lush glens, and gushing rivers.

It traverses some 42 km and was always intended as a romantic adventure. Along the way, there are many heritage features.

Convict graves dating back to the 1830s are found above the Explorers Tree. The abandoned mining village of Megalong is met beyond Nellies Glen. Remnant foundations and a line of trees are the only signs remaining. In central Megalong Valley an old cemetery may be visited. Set amongst the rough-barked angophoras on a grassy slope, the graves are ritually orientated east-west—in telling contrast to the disorder of the convict graves mentioned earlier.

The ruins of several settler's huts can be found near the Track. One, on the eastern bank of the Coxs River, is only recognisable by a line of abandoned fruit trees just above the small flood plain. These trees were an indispensable part of the settler's garden. In summer a short diversion from the track might yield a ripe piece of fruit, but don't be surprised if the fruit bats get there first!

Another site is found at remote Little River. As you pace the stony track, Little River's gurgling mountain waters divert your attention to a small sandstone outcrop on the grassy flat. There you'll see the remains of a large fireplace, with several other sandstone blocks nearby. It is so close to the river, and so low set, that floods would have been a greater danger than fire.

Old villages, ruins, lonely huts, mountains and rivers are all powerful ingredients of romanticism, and romance has always been part of the Track's history — even while it was still being built.

Work began on the Track in 1883 with a budget of £2500. The largest slice was spent close to Katoomba, constructing track down the luxuriant rainforest gully of Nellies Glen.

On the manner of its construction a newspaper reported:

> ...the passage was blocked by a huge boulder of some 1500 tons weight, which was lodged near the top...a heavy charge of dynamite caused it to burst up like a huge shell, which would put the products of Woolwich Arsenal in the shade. The mass went crashing down like an avalanche into the gully below...[1]

Despite this full-blooded approach—the romanticism of 'taming Nature'—construction took around three years. The rest of the trackmaking was slow but relatively simple, with most other work put into a bridle track to the Coxs River, up the Black Range, and into the final Caves descent.

Only four years before, the NSW government had gazetted coastal land south of Sydney as The National Park, making it the world's second declared national park. The government's less heralded Six Foot Track project involved only narrow strips of state lands, but late Victorian trackmaking lent it remarkable solidity. In Nellies Glen's narrow, rainforested gorge, for example, there remains the foundations of a footbridge over an extremely slight stream. As the track winds down to the Coxs River, contour-hugging tracks also display solidly reinforced embankments. Similar ones appear on the steeper descent to Jenolan Caves. Along its length the original trackmakers also nailed 88 evenly-spaced markers of white diamonds on canvas, replaced in later times by the tops of old kerosene tins.

The Times

The 1880s were energetic and affluent times in Australia. Wool-growing, cattle-raising, wheat-farming, dairying and fruit-growing were expanding industries. Overseas capital was prompting rapid development in gold, silver, copper and tin mining. There was a steady growth in professional, commercial and public services. With abundant resources, open spaces, and a white population of less than three million, the Australian states enjoyed healthy finances. Government funded not only economic development but also cultural, educational and recreational projects. Healthy recreational activities were gaining unprecedented acceptance.

There was much to be happy about: Australia was joined to Europe via cable communications; railways were expanding and steam trains were being introduced to Sydney; and gold, sheep, timber and other resources were rapidly being exploited. Self government was a reality in most colonies; the Chinese problem was being 'overcome' by a racially pure Australia; and Mechanical Institutes and Schools of Arts flourished.

The grand spirit appeared everywhere. When the railway joining Melbourne to Sydney was completed in 1883, the Melbourne *Argus* reported it:

> We have caught here somewhat of the spirit of the age, which is in favour of large and noble federations. Everywhere...men are drawn together...and they rejoice spontaneously, without affectation and without exception..

Within this cycle of wealth, Australians began to develop a sense of national identity. They relied less on imported culture and took an increasing interest in the things that made Australia different from the 'Old Country'—like kangaroos, merinos (not native, but numerous), gum trees and outback characters, all set in the wide open spaces of mountains and plains. Walking for pleasure was the best way of experiencing all of these things—and more.

Stories by Australians, about Australians and set in their own country were written and told, and photographic and painted images of native landscapes captured a local audience. A period of 'making Australia home' was pursued by former gold-diggers from a multitude of European countries—landowners and city folk alike.

Australia was experiencing its first taste of Romanticism—the most obvious ingredients of which were overseas influences and natural wonders like the mountains and the Jenolan Caves. The wonder of this is that it occurred only sixteen years after the last convict landed on Australian shores. Only a century after the first European settlement, Australia had been transformed from English dungeon to common man's throne.

The Jenolan Caves

> PWe are off to Jenolan. Everyone we meet bombards us with the question "Have you seen the Caves?" [2]

The Six Foot Track's rationale was the Jenolan Caves. The ornate limestone formations of the Elder, Lucas, Imperial, Left Imperial and Mammoth Caves, at one time internationally famous, stirred great excitement, particularly amongst the middle classes. Without this destination, the track would not have been built.

The caves already embodied a tale of rugged colonial romance. In the 1820s and 1830s, when cattle duffing flourished, outlaws rested and hid cattle in, or at, the caves. Safe from the searching eyes of the NSW constabulary in the deep gullies of the Fish River, surrounded by precipitous hills, the caves were an ideal hideaway.

In 1838 James and Charles Whalan, having captured an escaped convict there, returned later to discover the caves, which became known as the Fish River or Binda Caves[3]. Others were discovered in the 1840s. The place became a haven for visitors, its natural wonders repeatedly enthralling the public. Access was from the direction of Oberon, with visitors staying overnight on the Whalan's property.

During 1856 Jeremiah Wilson explored deep into the cave system discovering a splendid new cave, the Elder, which further increased public excitement. In 1860 he discovered the Lucas. By 1867 Wilson was appointed 'Keeper of the Caves', and was an acknowledged colonial hero and explorer.

For the clamouring public, reaching the Caves was also a matter of heroic proportions. From the north, access was won via Mt Victoria and the Binda cattle station, with passengers finally descending Mt George on horseback or foot. Travelling on a sometimes impassable horse and buggy track, the journey often took over 24 hours.

Other enthusiasts travelled by horseback or coach from Bathurst, Mt Victoria, Oberon, Hartley or Tarana. In the 1860s they would start from Sydney, staying overnight at Hartley or Bowenfels, before proceeding south. Once the railway reached Mt Victoria in 1868, local hotel owners constructed a track which ended two and a half kilometres from the caves. From there a steep horse track took visitors along the last leg.

Marked improvements occurred in 1872 when the railway reached Tarana, a settlement west of the caves. A short coach track from Tarana ended above the caves—this was rectified in 1879 and from then on the caves were accessible to all wishing to travel in comfort. Tarana appeared to be the natural departure point for all caves traffic.

The Role of Natural History

'The world is agog—for what? for bugs the size of Water Melons', said Audubon.

Parallelling the Cave's development was a booming Imperial interest in natural history. Popular books and magazines on the subject grew to unprecedented levels. In England *Common Objects of the Country* by the Rev. J.G. Wood sold 100 000 copies. Clubs and societies bristled with activities, often involving fieldwork in search of seaside species, ferns or Audubon's bugs. Preoccupation with the subject became intense because it was seen as 'good' and 'uplifting', not merely entertaining. At the time the natural sciences were closely associated with 'Natural Theology', which taught that all natural things brought us closer to God. Since every animal's behaviour in some way demonstrated God's purpose, or illustrated a moral Good, it was commonly felt that natural science elevated the mind. Not surprisingly, natural science was enthusiastically recommended for clergymen; but also for artisans and aristocrats, country dwellers and town dwellers; for ladies, children and old people—and all those who might otherwise hinder the course of business.

The popular passion for fieldwork led to the serious damage of Britain's flora and fauna. The almost inexplicable craze for fern collecting in the 1840s and 1850s led to the extinction of some species.

Imperial fashions always found their way to Australia and Jenolan Caves was soon affected. As Nature's 'bounty' appeared unending, visitors had a bad habit of taking souvenirs. In the early years, when the caves were poorly managed, the damage was extensive, an important motivation for the establishment of Jenolan Caves House.

The popularity of the caves created another problem: damage caused by carbon deposits left by lamp-lighting. This led to a another notable event: the early establishment of electric lighting within the caves in 1880, an achievement based on the colony's financial power.

By the 1870s the Cave's increased facilities, improved management and accessibility dramatically increased visitation. It had became one of the most popular attractions of inland Australia. After all these improvements the only thing missing was an adventurous way of getting there!

Katoomba

From the Katoomba end the Six Foot Track had a quite different story. Still a mining town in the 1880s, Katoomba was struggling to establish itself as tourist centre, with hoteliers particularly keen to transform it into a holiday Mecca. Who then had heard of Katoomba or the Three Sisters? Many more knew of Mt Victoria and Wentworth Falls.

Katoomba was adversely affected by the popularity of the Jenolan Caves. In a bid to tap this market and establish a leading position in the Blue Mountains, Harry Rowell of the Great Western Hotel lobbied for Katoomba as an alternative starting point for the caves. The Great Western was already a principal holiday destination for Sydney's upper classes, and it was here that the Premier, Sir Alexander Stuart, heard of the proposal for what became the Six Foot Track.

Within a year the Track's construction had begun. The only feasible route was through the steep terrain of Nellies Glen. A quick look at the map reveals one solid advantage: the route from Katoomba to the caves was the most direct. On a track suitable for both rider and walker, Megalong Valley was only four kilometres from Katoomba. By directly crossing the Coxs River, then moving up to and along the Black Range, the Track forms the third side of a simple triangle where the road system—then and now—forms the two other sides.

Of course the directness of the Track didn't change the fact that one had to either ride or walk all the way—and most people preferred wheeled transport.

Early Journeys

Although commercial motivation in Katoomba is sufficient explanation for the Track's development, it does not explain the Track's modest popularity. The initial decision for its construction was not prevented by parliamentary uproar or public outrage, nor did the Track fall into disuse. Why?

Hume Nisbet, an Australian artist, wrote 'As I turn away from the Caves...I now take the bridle track towards Katoomba, as I am told it is the most romantic and wildly imposing of the ways'.[4]

However what 'Irlswith' wrote in the *Sydney Mail* in 1884 is decidedly less romantic: 'until a halfway house can be erected, it would hardly be advisable for persons not tolerably certain of their staying powers to attempt it'. (It should be added that 'Irlswith' attempted the entire walk in one day.)

Romantics have always been more interested in the journey than in the destination, so the Six Foot Track was a first class opportunity for poetic travel. Here was grand country, wild and mountainous, and far from the dingy city office that epitomised the restrictions of the urban professions. People could follow the track on foot across rivers, through bushland and around paddocks, reflecting on the ways of the world.

But who were these people? Reviewing the surviving accounts of the Track the authors include members of a literary club, an editor, English globetrotters, a poet, a novelist, artists, scientists, prominent public servants and a naval officer—a fair cross section of middle class occupations. Perhaps members of the Warragamba Walking Club were typical. Their manual, *Swag and Billy* (1907), recommended that walkers carry the works of Byron, Keats, Tennyson, Wordsworth, Coleridge, Browning and Carlyle. Others were more influenced by Ruskin and William Morris. Doesn't the harshness of Australia as depicted in *His Natural Life* seem light years away?

Other Early Accounts

'Irlswith' fell short of completing the walk in one day by only three kilometres.

Perhaps he spent too much time making copious notes, as his description of Little River is engaging:

> ...In the centre of this..stood a tall black bearded man, the tatty picturesqueness of whose attire was heightened by a red scarf around his neck...On the bank of the creek was a bark hut, at a little distance off the ashes and smoke of a fire, a woman seated on a log, and two horses tethered to a tree...

Here Romanticism takes the form of the picturesque, allied with the gallantry of walking the Track solo.

In 1886 members of the Pickwick Club, all named after Dicken's characters, decided to take 'ladies' on the walk. What followed was

> months of preparation...despite the dire warnings of many people...that all manner of difficulties would occur along the way, in the shape of thunderstorms, rivers too high...snakes...snowstorms, want of water, tight boots, teeth aching, cold, heat, wild dogs, bulldog ants, spiders, no tracks, blackfellows...etc.[5]

In an 1890s account writer, poet and journalist John Le Gay Brereton walked the Track as part of a longer journey: from Gladesville (in Sydney) to Katoomba, then to Jenolan Caves, Wombeyan Caves, Moss Vale, Kangaroo Valley, Kiama and back to Sydney, a large circle of perhaps 500 km. Published as *Landlopers* (1899) it whimsically reflects on his entry to Megalong Valley:

> As we swing gaily across the undulating country which forms the bottom of the Valley, we are greeted at every step with cries of welcome from all kinds of birds. Parrots of various species screamed and chattered, and magpies carolled in the trees. As we were passing a piece of swampy ground, three spur-wing plovers ran off, cackling. The kookaburras burst into long peals of laughter. I laughed too, wildly and plenteously, to the amazement of The Boy, who asked, "What's the joke?" And...I shouted 'Life!'...

Here is unbridled romanticism!

The early guidebooks also joined in: 'The scenery en route is most rewarding.' (Woolcott, 1888); 'The wildest and most picturesque route.'(Foster, 1890); 'The romantic beauty of the surroundings amply compensates for the roughness of the ground.' (*Railway Guide*, 1897)

Here, romanticism is an emotional state induced by natural beauty.

However the record of Dowdy's trip in February, 1912 shows a more sobering, though sometimes comic, dimension.[6]

> Hearing on all sides that the Blue Mountains would not be properly 'done' without a visit to the world famous Jenolan Caves, and the Guide Book and Tourist Map clearly state that 'the Track is good and well defined, and there are several settlers along the Track', my wife & I thought we would spend a pleasant weekend by walking to Jenolan: Our luggage consisted of night clothing only, and our ration of four pears and two lemons, as we counted on being able to procure from one or more of the 'several settlers' any meals that we should want en route.

Poor Dowdy and wife endured a whole catalogue of disasters, including heat, thirst, hunger, bushfire and finding nowhere to stay. They sought aid from several settlers, only to find nobody home! Finally, having limped back to civilisation (Blackheath) and treated themselves to food, baths and sleep, Dowdy offers this advice: 'To anyone who thinks of essaying a similar walk my advice is don't—unless accompanied by a guide, swag, and plenty of provisions...And whatever you do, put no trust in guidebooks'.

To this, what can an author of guidebooks say?

The Track's popularity continued in the Federation years with accounts in guide booklets, magazines and newspapers. Track descriptions were included in Tricketts *Guide to the Jenolan Caves* (1899) and *The Mountaineer Tourist Guide* (1904).

Tompkins's book, *With Swag and Billy* (1907,1914), probably the first guidebook on recreational walking in NSW, gives a further account of the walk. He comments on the track's broad appeal, with 'the interest taken in walking by ladies...remarkable'. His special advice on 'Walking for Ladies' appears in the second and third editions, replacing the previous edition's reflections on choosing accompanying literature! Moreover Tompkins comments positively (if paternally) on female involvement in trekking:

> As we make our way through the scented woodland the girls form the advance guard, tripping along expectantly, chatting merrily, and feeling that it is a joy to be alive; the men smoke, and bring up the rear—and most of the baggage. To observe the zest with which the girls enter the more or less common incidents by the way—epoch making events to them—is to be rejuvenated.

Brereton's groundbreaking *Landlopers* idealised the Australian countryside and the act of walking through it. On his sojourn Brereton carried Walt Whitman's 'Leaves of Grass', a classic 'declaration of freedom' through personal communion with nature. The influence is apparent in his poetry:

> In the thickly wooded valleys are a thousand merry calls,
> that echo in the Warragamba heart;
> The voice of the rushing winds and filmy waterfalls,
> Are louder than the hucksters of the mart.
>
> We leave a drink untasted on the swell Australian bar,
> And dream of some sequestered wooden pub;
> We are pagans—for the tolling chapel bells are fainter far,
> Than the singing of the bellbirds in the scrub.
>
> A thousand homes are waiting us by gully, plain and hill,
> A thousand fireless altars wait unseen;
> But tomorrow you may follow us on any track you will
> By the little patch of black upon the green.
>
> For clad in love and sunlight goes the leader of the clan,
> The trappings of modernity are shed.
> while Tompkins bangs his brolly on his polished frying pan,
> or waves his carpet slippers 'round his head.[7]

The Decline of the Track

World War I (1914-18) marked the end of the Track's romantic period. Later usage rose and fell with the decades. Popularity was briefly renewed in the early 1920s, and again during the depression years, but both romance and romantics appeared to have died.

Documented accounts are thin. 'The Black Rangers' (1921), an eight-page pamphlet, is the last fresh account. They found the Track 'greatly overgrown with bracken and other growth'. More persistent were the tourist guides, like *New Walks and Sights: Katoomba and Leura* (1928) Penfold's (1930s), Miles, Melville and Quigley's. All were merely whole or partial reprints of past accounts. It is as if the first post-war decade was attempting to recreate the past.

Miles's 1932 description was the last to encourage walkers to use the track. Entitled 'Route from Katoomba or Blackheath' it reads:

> ...it is very rough and should not be attempted except by those thoroughly used to long walking tours. There is no accommodation...and in places water is difficult to obtain. Those...anxious to take this route...are advised to form a party under an experienced leader...and take sufficient water and provisions for a full journey...

This decline in written works may be partly explained by walking's new found popularity amongst the less educated or affluent. Walking was a cheap means of recreation, so its appeal increased in the depression years.

The post World War II years were the Track's lowest ebb. The 4wd vehicle, which so many soldiers had learnt to drive, was turned to defeat another, dark enemy: the bush. The western world's cycle of wars had left the population longing for domesticity and affluence, and bushfires sometimes threatened both. A fire trail mania grew, with vehicular tracks constructed along every possible ridge. In this way a large slice of the Track, most of Jenolan Caves to Mini Mini saddle, was turned into road. Walker access remained, but the Track's charm was sorely compromised.

In the mid-sixties there was another assault on the Track. The Blue Mountains Council proceeded with a harebrained proposal to construct a road down Nellies Glen. Despite an average gradient of 1:2.5, with one steep section of 1:1.75 (Mt Victoria Pass is 1:6.8) which was pointed out by engineers the authorities persisted. The resulting piece of official vandalism scarred the Glen's beauty. The results can still be seen today.

In the same decade the Council 'upgraded' to vehicular standards sections of the Track from the Coxs River to Mini Mini saddle, and along the Megalong Valley road to the edge of Nellies Glen. There remained only 5 to 6 km of the original track.

Accounts of the walk grew sparse; the next main account wasn't published until 1967. The trail markers had gradually disappeared. The track had become indistinct, particularly where it passed through private properties. Another 16 years passed before Jim Smith's account of his walk with Wilf Hilder. The Track was on the brink of disintegration.

Reopening the Six Foot Track

Renewed interest in Australian heritage and the environment gave Jim Smith, Wilf Hilder and others with an active regional interest, a platform and opportunity to draw public attention to the Track's condition. Unless reconstruction was commenced the Track would be permanently lost

Lands Department involvement saved the Track from obscurity. Fortunately the department was just becoming involved again with recreational walking projects after a long absence 'from the field'. Once the most powerful state government department, it still had human and budgetary resources at its disposal, neatly coinciding with community demands.

On an individual level Alan Carey from the Orange Lands Office, played a significant role in the Track's reconstruction. He had earlier been involved in the 1979 reopening of Mt York heritage tracks. These colonial, and Federation, roads had been constructed as alternatives to Victoria Pass.

Politically, the swelling interest in the environment, local affairs and heritage reached its first peak with the Whitlam government; but even after the dismissal of the government in 1975, community commitment to the environment continued to increase. What changed was the economic circumstances; harder times forced a new ethos—we had to make better use of existing resources. The Six Foot Track was just such a resource. Reconstruction was timed for reopening in the Track's centennial year, 1984.

Early Track Usage

Jim Smith estimates that 10 000 people walked the Track over the years between 1884 and 1921[8]. This is calculated on recorded or published accounts over those years. However conclusions about the Track's early popularity are conjectural, with approximations of usage necessarily treated with caution. Authoritative records were never kept.

Modern Usage

Today the Track is more popular than ever, and why not? The 1880s grand landscape is still there; the rocky, cascading waters of the Coxs River beckons us, while Nellies Glen, despite assault in the 1960s, still has dramatic appeal. Add the remarkable and pleasing descent to Jenolan Caves and the challenge of the climb to the Black Range, and you have sufficient ingredients for a worthwhile, scenic journey.

Most weekends see a wide range of users from mountain bike riders, day walkers, overnight walkers, running enthusiasts and trekkers traversing part or all of the Track. Less welcome trail biker riders also use it (riding trail bikes is not allowed on the private property sections of the Track).

Originally designed for both horseriders and walkers, it is now unsuitable for horseriders, but horseriders are well catered for in other parts of the Megalong Valley.

Today's usage is probably greater than ever before.[9] During peak track use some 30 people might be met over a three day walk, most on either side of the Coxs River. On long weekends there may be as many as 15 to 20 people starting the walk at Explorers Tree—not counting our groups. It is quite common to meet a cluster of scouts or guides—and others—walking from Jenolan State Forest to Katoomba. In the colder months—June to August—fewer people may be met. As guides on the Six Foot Track we usually start the walk on Saturday mornings, so Sunday's walkers to the Coxs River are avoided—we'd already be in the more remote Little River region.

To this formula add 200 people who annually join our 'no backpacking' walks[10], throw in an unknown number of runners practising or participating in the marathon—up to 100, or even 200?—and we have the raw basis for calculations. Cling-clang! It amounts to approximately 1000 doing a weekend or extended walk; with another 2000+ doing a day or return overnight walk to the Coxs' River. Assuming constant use over the last three years the area has seen 9000 to 12 000 walkers, of which perhaps 1000 would have completed the entire journey.

The Return of Romanticism?

This prompts a final question: does the re-opening of the Track indicate a new, leaner, era of romanticism?

Let's first sweep away the preconception that we are talking of a return to romanticisms of yesteryear. Those are gone; killed off by war, depression and disillusionment. Conceptions of the sublime and the transcendent are far from the thoughts of today's walkers. They do not hope to reach ethereal heights by communing with nature with the help of appropriate literature. Perhaps only traditionalist walking clubs and a few eccentrics, bless their hearts, still carry literature at all.

We have already discovered one reason for this change. Men and women now walk together. In an all-male group speed is usually the imperative, not the sublime. So perhaps the poetry, the romance lies elsewhere...

So what other values might constitute a late 20th century romanticism? We have been going through economic recession, which tends to force people back on their own resources. As a consequence domestic life again has a central place in our culture, and outdoor activities are a part of this. Environmental appreciation is firmly established and accepted by all shades of government. Also, people value acting locally. Today, when the environment is under attack, everyone knows it.

The environment and economy have been centre stage for almost two decades. The conflict of conservationist and forestry interests has created an ongoing national drama. With a new awareness of the natural environment people are keen to appreciate it while it's still there. We are encouraged to adventure by all those who dearly love it. If there is romanticism it lies in people's involvement in the big questions of life, liberty and planet, in participating in the 'good fight'.

Romanticism's other ideal concerns the body. Bushwalking provides challenge, self-sufficiency and food for the imagination. Beach culture, that other competitor for challenge and sense of achievement has been taken over by commercialism. What better challenge, what better involvement in harmless exercise and recreation, than bushwalking? It is cheaper than skiing, safer than walking the streets, and one place where you can still breathe deeply.

But who does these walks? Scouts, guides and cubs are introduced to the mountains by their volunteer leaders. Marathon enthusiasts run the Track every year. Others venture the overnight walk to the Coxs River and back. Daytrippers take a stroll down Nellies Glen. Then there is the occasional fishing trip, annual picnic or meander around the caves from the Binda huts. Some take up the full challenge of completing the entire walk.

These walks are not without incident. Only a year ago two people were lifted out of Little River by helicopter, suffering from severe frostbite and hunger. Others have met the occasional fury of a flooding Coxs River, while breaking a leg, meeting fire or roadside snakes are other dangers. While guide books no longer promise 'a few settlers along the way', unpreparedness is still commonplace. One group recently took no wet weather gear with them, and paid the price.

Is this the stuff of Romance? Yes, the Track still has inherently romantic content: the grandeur of the mountains and atmospheric weather patterns. Yes, there is the challenge, the pleasures, the rewards of trekking. Yes, the great question of our relationship with our surroundings is a modern drama. But the final ingredient is this: walking the Track embeds us all in our history, the track is a lasting reminder of Australia's earliest brush with Romanticism.

Walking the Six Foot Track

By the hardened bushwalker's standards the Six Foot Track has never been ideal. It has alway been a 'half civilised' Track. It crosses numerous private properties and is outside the more remote areas of the Blue Mountains. From the 1950s much of the original route was obscured by fire trail. The growth of the NSW National Parks system bypassed the Track, which only just borders the Kanangra-Boyd NP.

The Track's popularity stems partly from easy accessibility by train, bus and car. For those with cars there are six entry points: Nellies Glen, Megalong Valley, Black Range, Jenolan State Forest, Kiora Hill and Jenolan itself—all suitable for weekend walking. (See Access map).

Those using public transport have options too. You could catch a train to Mt Victoria, then 'bus' to Jenolan State Forest for a weekend walk, returning to Katoomba. Or start from Nellies Glen, camp at Coxs River, then return. Most of the Track can be traversed over a weekend, perhaps ending at Jenolan State Forest and connecting with the return bus. The dedicated, and fit, can walk the lot, but for most this is not recommended!

Variable paces can be accommodated. Daywalks, weekend camping and trekking are all possible, whether at a speedy, or rambling pace. The Coxs River day walk from Megalong Valley is particularly popular and takes in some of the remaining original track. Many people stroll down Nellies Glen, then do either the return climb or continue to Megalong Valley Rd. The 'speed freaks' of the walking fraternity occasionally attempt the Track in 24 hours. The marathon run record for the Track is a remarkable three hours and twelve minutes!

However, for a gentle, romantic walk, a few notes on the Track may help the less experienced walker.

Seasonal factors are most important in the mountains. In summer give all your attention to detail: the sun and the heat are unforgiving enemies. Get that broad rimmed hat on, and keep it on; use the sunscreen; turn up collars for extra protection; dampen a handkerchief, tie it around your neck and enjoy it. Take every opportunity to walk in shade, and rest regularly (in shade). Get yourself wet at every opportunity—don't be squeamish about water or wetness, it's the best antidote to heat. Carry a good supply of water; at least two—but preferably three—litres.

Just as too little water has an undesirable affect, so does having too much. Excessive water is effectively a poison, so the body rejects it—and the contents of your stomach! So summer walkers shouldn't guzzle water; they should spread it throughout the day. Dry lips mislead many a walker: it is no indication of thirst, just lips dried by heat and/or wind, easily solved with your mouth's moisture (or take a lip salve).

In other seasons the great dangers are lack of food and weather variations. Two walkers suffering from frostbite and hunger were recently lifted out by helicopter, an embarrassing and ignominious rescue from a track so close to properties.

Winter can be cold but people greatly underrate it. Too many people avoid it as a time to walk. In fact it can be ideal—you'll be kept warm by the activity of walking, and your exposed face will enjoy the cool air.

Because of the long nights a few extra precautions need to be taken:

1. Walk shorter distances, or keep a steady pace with short breaks. Calculate your walking time so you're not caught short of camp in the dark.
2. Take extra warm clothing and provide for a decent fire.
3. Dare I say it—take a few stories in your head and a book in your pack. Read aloud!

Remember too that from July to November rainfall is usually low.

Spring is a favourite time to walking the Track. You'll find waratahs, orchids and rock lilies, especially in late spring. The base of Nellies Glen is especially rewarding from October.

Wildlife

A diverse wildlife still occupies the region, but by day it is not always apparent. Black snakes and goannas are common, with many small insects, lizards and butterflies worth a closer look.

One little known joy of a summer walk is the thousands of butterflies found as you climb from Little River to Black Range. They are hidden in the shade of the fire trail's embankment. As you pass close to the embankment the disturbed butterflies will give you a kaleidoscopic experience.

At dusk wallabies or lyrebirds may be seen. Long periods of shooting at both have made them flee at short notice. In former years both were numerous.

At night sugar gliders, ringtail possums, wombats, fruit bats and (perhaps) the quoll can be spotted. Spotlighting for these and other animals will reward at almost any point along the Track.

Accommodation

There are many places where you can camp along the Six Foot Track and in the general area. There is a camping ground at Little River and there are also sites on the western side of the Coxs River; where the Track meets the Jenolan Caves road; and at Jenolan itself. There are also several places where you can camp on the Black Range. Try to camp where others have already built fireplaces.

For a more comfortable stay, there are the Binda Huts on Mt George, 5 km before the Caves, and if you are opting for luxury, there is of course Caves House.

Maps

It is tempting to leave behind detailed maps; those strange topographic lines are a mystery, the cliff lines seem all too obvious, and names are probably the most useless fact of all. It's no secret that the track is largely easy to follow.

However a map can also an informative and entertaining beast, and can help you start to discover and understand the area.

You can enjoy meandering around a map, locating something of note, and if you are uneasy with the thought of using maps, you probably need one!

The reason why you should take a map is simple—one mistake can ruin a walk.

The 1:25000 maps covering the Six Foot Track are Katoomba, Hampton and Jenolan. Otherwise write away for the Dept of Conservation and Land Management (formerly the Lands Dept) brochure. It is quite sufficient for most people.

Acknowledgment

Much of the history of the Six Foot Track given in this chapter is based on the research of Jim Smith and Wilf Hilder found in *From Katoomba to Jenolan Caves*. It is used by permission of the copyright holder, Jim Smith, and the publisher, Second Back Row Press.

Footnotes

1 Smith, Jim. *From Katoomba to Jenolan Caves*. Second Back Row Press, 1984, p.8.

2 'Our Holiday Resorts', *Illustrated Sydney News,* 1889. (Reprinted in Smith, 1984, p.36).
3 See also Historical Notes on the Six Foot Track, pub. by the Dept of Conservation and Land Management.
4 Smith, 1984, p.32.
5 Smith,1984, p.27.
6 *Sydney Mail*, 6/3/1912 (reprinted in Smith, 1984, p.57).
7 From a 1907 letter in the Warragamba Walking Club Song Book.
8 Smith, 1984, p.112.
9 My estimate of present usage is based on my own, and two other guides' observations over a three year period.
10 Via our 4wd-supported walks. For more information, contact 'Great Australian Walks', ph. 555 7580.

The Historic Corn Trail

Before the 1830s, Australia's only large settlements were Sydney and Hobart, 1500 kilometres apart. Both had been established for less than 50 years. In the outlands only small and scattered settlements and (usually illegal) 'runs' existed.

Without declared settlement boundaries the government found its rule thwarted, so in 1829 Governor Darling restricted settlement to the 'Nineteen Counties', naming them after familiar English counties like Cumberland. Settlers could only acquire land within a radius of approximately 240 km of Sydney; an area bounded by the Manning River in the north, the Mooruya River in the south and the Lachlan in the west. By 1831 there were to be no more land grants.

In fact expansion continued. Reckless, adventurous and land-hungry men moved out to districts such as the Monaro Plains (around present day Braidwood)—not so much to cultivate land as to run cattle and sheep. It was wild country, and the dispossessed Aborigines frequently harassed the newcomers.

There was also the transport problem. Wagon tracks to Sydney were either too rough, unreliable, slow or just non-existent. The coastal link, as incredible as it seems today, was the more viable route. Small coastal ships carrying produce from Sydney were the major means of distributing merchandise, and of course there was no shortage of able seamen in the colony.

The southern highlands squatters had no access to this coastal trade, so a reliable route from Braidwood to the coast was vital.

East of Canberra lies the 'Optimists' section, where the southern highlands drop rapidly to the coastal forests and plains. It is so named because anyone who thought to put a road through here was dubbed an optimist!

Like so many earlier settlers, who had tried and failed, some of those optimists set about making that link—and succeeded.

Built in the 1830s, the 'Corn Trail' (as it is now called) provided two-way benefits: for Bolero Valley farmers, it was a means of transporting produce to the highlanders; for the highlanders, it was a link to Bateman's Bay and, via shipping, the Sydney market.

Mountain Grey Gum, Messmate, Ribbon Gum
R2 Mountain Grey Gum, Roughbarked Apple, River Peppermint, Yellow Stringybark

Dry Rainforest
DR Grey Myrtle

Warm Temperate Rainforest *WTR*

Sunnypatch
SP Kurrajong, Brush Kurrajong, Late Black Wattle, Black She Oak, Peach Loaf Poison Bush, Hazel Pomaderis, Native Olive, Mint Bush, Port Jackson Fig

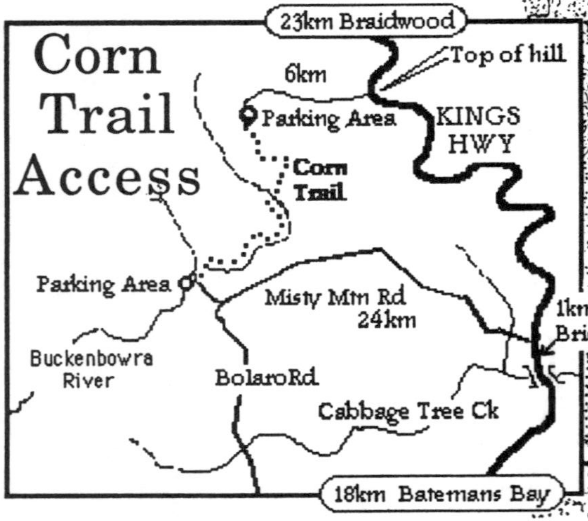

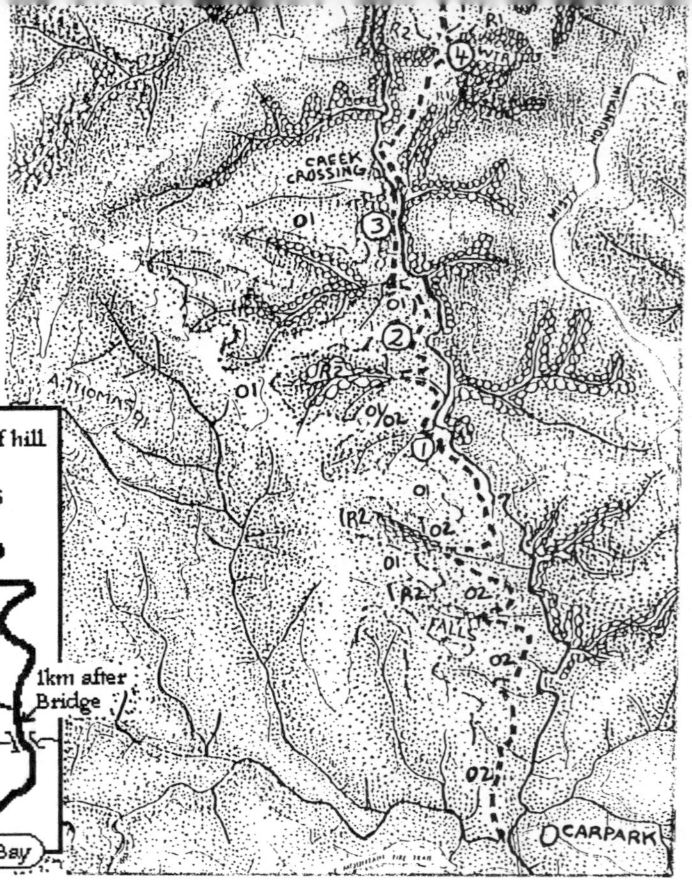

The Corn Trail

Map Key

- - - - - - Corn Trail
. . . . . . former route (no longer exists)
88888 WTR rainforest

① Sunnypatch : SP
② Side cut across clifftop : O1 above, R2 below
③ Cabbage Fan Palms : large Silky River Oaks, WTR
④ Spur to gully : U1, O2, R1, WTR
⑤ Saddle at end of switchbacks. Grades ease as trail traverses north slope of rocky knob through a stand of Black Oaks and U1
⑥ The Knoll : regrowth after severe wildfire
⑦ Water gum grove
⑧ Stone cairn : U1, Blackboys

Open Forest
O1 Silvertop Ash
O2 Mountain Grey Gum, Roughbarked Apple, Stringybarks, Bloodwood
O3 White Ash, Brown Barrell, Ribbon Gum, Gully Peppermint

Upland Woodland
U1 Silvertop Ash

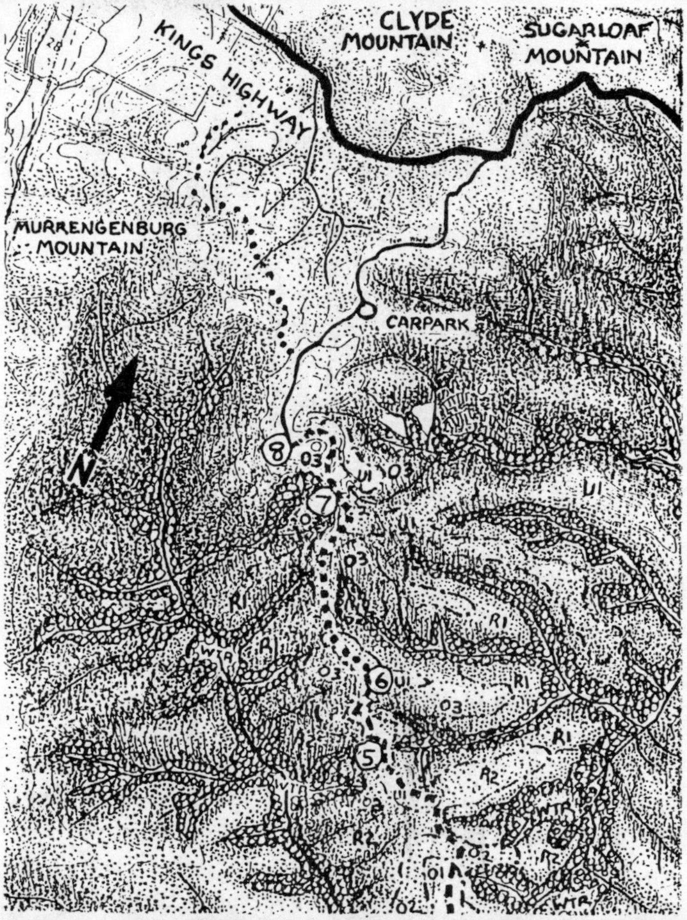

The major crop carried inland was corn, grown in the valleys and transported by pack-horses, which were usually led by the womenfolk of the pioneer families. A shed was built at the top of the mountain. From here, carts would transport produce to the towns of Braidwood and Araluen. In the other direction cattle were driven down from the tablelands for coastal agistment and sale. Gold prospectors, hopeful of striking it rich along the Buckenbowra River and at Araluen, also used the Corn Trail.

In 1854 another route was opened over the Clyde Mountain, roughly following the present Kings Highway. The Corn Trail went into gradual decline. By the 1920s it had become completely overgrown. Its last usage was during World War II, when the Army reconnoitred the trail, searching for additional routes over the mountain in case of enemy invasion.

Interest in the Corn Trail led a local group of historians to research, plot and reconstruct the trail using a 1987 grant from the Bicentennial Authority. The result is a 12.5 km section of track running from Murrengenburg Mountain (800 m ASL) through virgin forest, to the head of the Bolero Valley (150 m ASL). The Corn Trail is now accessible to all.

Walking the Trail

The Corn Trail is about 22 km west of Bateman's Bay, which is on the South Coast about three and a half hours' drive from Sydney. To reach the Trail, take the Kings Hwy (between Bateman's Bay and Braidwood). The signposted turnoff is on top of Murrengenburg Mountain.

The following description follows the Trail from bottom (the Buckenbowra River) to top (Murrengenburg Mtn). Most people walk from top to bottom, so my description is a challenge to walkers!

If you do begin on the Buckenbowra River (see map for access), the Corn Trail consists of two parts: along the river's upper reaches, where the Trail follows the contours and thus climbs gradually; followed by the steep, mountainous pass towards Murrengenburg Mountain. Most is within Buckenbowra State Forest (BSF) and is remarkably well preserved after more than a century's disuse.

There is space to camp at the top and bottom of the Trail. You can also camp midway on the Trail, but the whole Trail can be easily walked in a day.

The upper Buckenbowra River is a small meandering stream set deep in a gully—an enchanting setting. The valley slopes are moderately steep, and are densely forested on the lower parts. The river is fringed with casuarinas, which share the creek banks with rainforest and eucalypt species, all bustling for light.

The beds of rounded river stones, and the small pools give the river an unmistakable character.

A 'modern' cairn leads the walker onto the track.

On my first visit, I wondered whether the track downstream had been obliterated by time or forestry activities. So I wandered back to see. On examination it appeared to meander along the stream as best it could. Sometimes the track was overgrown, at other times, it became merely part of forestry road. Disappointing.

On returning, something caught my attention: a large stone tablet. There were no obvious words on it, but a deep vertical mark ran down one side. Perhaps there was something on the opposite side? Unfortunately it was buried too deeply, with other rocks, sand and vegetation around, and it was too large to budge. My curiosity would have to remain unsatisfied.

On the first stretch of the Trail it's single file past a forest thicket and tree ferns to the first water crossing, where one creek meets another. Above this point the Buckenbowra and an adjoining stream part company—all the better for crossing.

It's summer, so few stepping stones are needed to save the walker getting wet feet. (Personally I take every opportunity to get wet, especially in summer!). Nearby is an elegant grevillea, long leafed and slightly jagged. I'm not qualified to identify it, but there is a strong resemblance to the rare *Grevillea shireii* of the Hawkesbury area, far to the north.

The track then follows the Buckenbowra. A large cairn, encrusted with lichen, moss and the occasional fern, appears unmoved for 160 years. The way ahead bisects the two streams and zigzags upwards through a dark enclave, the only section of 'dry' rainforest along the entire track. On both sides, moss banks cover tree roots. Wispy native grass clumps grow happily. Here amongst the grey myrtles is a place to linger, perhaps making an additional sally up the other stream.

Higher up is open forest where silvertop ash, mountain grey gum and bloodwoods dominate. The burrawangs and tall grass clumps dot the forest floor. Fallen logs and small animal burrows from last night's diggings are the local events. One old log had scattered chips around it, evidence of the marsupial burrowing that aids the complete breakdown of wood to soil.

Here and there are lopped trees and overgrown ground cuttings, leftovers of previous forestry activity. Even an overgrown forestry road can be spotted across the track. It's January, but there are still three or four lily species blooming.

Above the river the track, like all good horse trails (as the Corn Trail originally was, of course), follows the contours. It winds back and forth, skirting the first rainforest gully.

Cabbage-tree palms, burrawang, tree ferns and native raspberry share the same ground, Sassafras and river peppermints are overhead. Above sounds the 'k-ar k-ar k-ar' and 'k-ee-ee k-ee-ee' of the black cockatoo—like the odd, rasping sound of wine being uncorked, before the 'pop'.

The track is occasionally overgrown, with drooping ferns, grasses and vines.

Modern track makers have snipped the sharp-edged burrawang fronds where they cover the track, a necessary measure for safe walking. Since the burrawang averages only one new frond per season, it will be slow to reclaim the trail.

After 30 minutes on this early colonial track the lungs and legs pump easily. What could be more enjoyable than walking this track's contour-hugging, stone-lined route? On such a well-used track, the cairns are set at regular intervals—creating a reassuring metre. Each is a reminder that all is well. The track is natural and, in the best sense, unremarkable.

Open forest soon takes over again, this time in stands of stringybark and messmate. The grassy undergrowth must be attractive fodder for the wallaby. The track continues to be clear and easy walking.

Around a third gully the track passes above a small waterfall. Adjacent is an angular outcrop of schist. Streaky, and adorned with palm frond, this rock is a reminder of the area's violent geological past.

There are tree ferns in the next gully too. Each one over three metres in height is remarkable for its thickened base. Some of the blackened trunks have epiphytes attached; others are adorned with grass skirts. At this point you can spot an original trail cutting, over 100 metres long, and one of the first sections discovered during reconstruction.

Back in the open forest again my earlier speculation is confirmed; wallabies do graze here. Five or six flee wildly from the forest floor, past the thin bushes to the safety of closed forest. Hearing them is easy; observing more than their tails is ambitious! The gun has long established their fear of humanity.

Evidence of other animals appears too; the odd wombat's hole, the diggings of lyrebirds and small marsupials. Nearby are pigeons and small forest birds foraging on the forest floor.

Shoulder to shoulder with the mountains now, the creek below, I keep up a smooth pace. A feeling of well-being passes through me: the morning light filters through the pure stands of silvertop ash; the whiff of eucalypt is a delight and ahead lies a well lit path through history. The smooth path following the contours of the slope, the sound of tumbling waters below—everything instils a welcome sense of remoteness; and it is an added pleasure to walk on a track so well preserved, so free of erosion.

A curious feature appears: a tree fern colony running downhill across the usual ecological divide. About 50 metres above is a group of tree ferns and, as if seeds had been scattered downhill, a long succession of their offspring runs down the slope, across the track, and down to the river's edge like the contents of a parcel, accidentally dropped.

Immediately after this is a line of stone cairns spaced every five metres or so. There must be a dozen or more. Odd, as previous cairns have occurred either at strategic points or 'every so often'. There is nothing apparently unusual about this particular place, no real need for the reassurance they usually imply. The track's direction is in no doubt; yet here they are.

Nearby is an open slope known as the Sunny Patch. A basaltic soil type has given it a distinctive combination of native species, unfortunately sorely tested by past stock grazing. Where the ground has been disturbed and is revegetating, I spot patches of Scotch thistle and other exotics.

At last a familiar distraction—a leech, the first in one and a half hours—off you go, fella! Somewhere to my left comes a strange bird call reminiscent of a 1950s 'mug lair'. I look hard but can't see its 'mug' anywhere. And—hello, hello—a felled rough-barked angophora, less sensual and elegant than the *Costata* species (wrongly called Sydney red gum) but its branches are just as amazingly contorted.

Aged tree ferns occupy the next slope. Many are 'double-headers', i.e. they have two heads growing from the same trunk. A 40-header has been recorded in WA. Most reach three to four metres in height. Just here the trail enforces a straight path, like a church aisle. It takes time to realise that a remarkable number of the tree ferns have been felled. But by whom? Several trunks appear to taper off; perhaps they've been destroyed by fire. Others have splintered, possibly by the weight of age. But some can not be explained, so I leave puzzled, but suspect the worst. A lyrebird lets out one of its natural, (not imitative), calls. Bird nest ferns are sighted at last.

Soon a reconstructed cutting appears, the first obvious sign of modern track making. Here the track must have disintegrated where it skirted a steep embankment, as workers have made a clean cut across it. For the first time the track passes along a steep hillside, and time has seen it collapse. I speculate that past track builders had a purpose in common with the modern builders—a determination to avoid retreat down the slope, followed by an equal return climb. The route chosen adds to the walk's smoothness.

At this point, the track makers had not yet got to the route's 'business end'—the steep climb up Murrengenburg Mountain. From Bateman's Bay (or an upstream port) they'd probably used existing track (either pastoral or Aboriginal), then extended it upstream, encountering all the accompanying difficulties of dependence on the river's 'temper'. From where we joined the Buckenbowra the track makers had found it practical to stay above the stream, but this has also had the effect of introducing more variety into the route, and the journey. It is now, as it would have been then, pleasant for both human and horse to traverse.

Such speculating absorbs me on this sunny morning. Straight through a seventh gully I walk. A multitude of bird-calls echo down the gully. Ground parrots appear, as usual, in pairs. Rhythm has taken over as I tramp through the now familiar open forest. But I see something that, despite this rhythm, stops me in my tracks: an eighth gully.

In truth this gully is magical. In front of me a flat expanse of lowland—gully's end, or river flat, I can't tell—while to my left is a giant casuarina, its trunk resembling a Moreton Bay fig. Before me are multitudes of tree ferns. Casuarina needles adorn their fronds, and mat the floor. These ferns are *Cyathea antarcticus* (soft-barked fern). Never have I seen so many in one place: hundreds spread before me as far as the eye can see.

Stillness prevails, the light is subdued. Here and there are the healthiest young cabbage tree palms; most are quite low-growing with extravagant fronds. The older ones touch the ground. Further up the gully are giant stinging trees, sassafras, lilly pilly and churnwood. I am lost in admiration of the scene.

For a time the track disappears. I follow an opening which I hope is correct. About 100 metres across this beautiful scene I stumble into a stony terrain of scrubby, retarded vegetation—a shocking case of 'beauty and the beast'.

Somewhere nearby is a campsite and staging area for the steep climb ahead. The sound of flowing water grows louder, beckoning me. Down an embankment, and I've finally arrived. I throw down my pack, take a gulp of refreshing water, and relax. So ends stage one of the Corn Trail.

The mountain climb lies ahead, but before this, it's worth noting the stream's nearby pools. On many a day it's good enough for a delightful wade. I mention it because the 'lazy walker' could happily walk this contoured track, have lunch and a swim, then return along the same path. The 'typical' walker will walk top to bottom!

A warning here. This is probably the only place where the novice can get lost. After crossing the creek the track appears to climb over an embankment and into canopy rainforest, and from the signs, walkers seem to have done exactly that—fatal! The sharp left turn immediately after the embankment is easily missed—you are warned!

So, faithful walker, take the sharp left turn and follow the track upstream. Be impressed by the parasitic fig tree—it is old and established, yet is itself being worn down by nine or so weighty birds nest ferns. As well, coachwood, sassafras, giant stinging trees, grey myrtle and others contribute to the subdued light.

A few hundred metres later the climb begins. The trail shrewdly aligns itself with an upturn schist strata. 'Here goes', I think, regretfully, 'away from the beloved environs of the stream'. The zigzag begins, and continues. The track is moderately sloped—a relief—but it is also relentless.

Grass trees abound, the sun's rays beat down. I keep to the shade, turn up the collar, cover the sunny side of my body and expose the other. Wet towels are a blessing.

As the walk progresses through open woodland it becomes apparent that the climb is staged in 'shoulders'. With such thin undergrowth it is possible to see as far as the slope's edge. But the only sign of reaching the top of the shoulder is an easing of the track's incline. Immediately after, another shoulder follows. So the walk can be staged by resting on each shoulder.

Along the way the track's excellent state of preservation is amazing. It is largely intact and still stone-lined, traversing country not yet breached by forestry activity; no clearances, lopped trees or stumps.

I am walking in dry summer conditions. Leaf litter is thick on the ground, fallen trees and smaller branches abound. A droopy calliptis (native pine) shows the stress of the dry weather.

What lies ahead? Another shoulder of course! The track winds anti-clockwise along the eastern face, sunny side up. By now I am familiar with the early track makers' methods: basically track making by sight!

In the open surrounds of dry sclerophyll country the track cuts a steady incline up and around the shoulder. But as soon as a vertical wall of rainforest (shown as 4 on the map hand-drawn by Alan Thomas) is within sight, the track turns sharp left and winds uphill, now running clockwise. It is to happen again and again.

What is there to see? I spot a huge, spongy lichen. It is wet, and about 30 centimetres in diameter—an upturned white carcass. On the rounded open slopes, pure stands of blackened eucalypts—fire-licked silvertop ash. Their trunks, singed from one to four metres above ground, stand otherwise unaffected. With the setting of rounded, dry hills, this is classic Fred Williams material.

Walking through this landscape, the track steering a steady course, I feel a sailor's sentiment stirring: steady as she goes, mate, steady as she goes. I'm in my stride again. When the track flattens out a little, I find myself turning bosun, saying 'Don't you dare go down!' Even now, after almost an hour's climb, the tributary steam is audible, visible and still all too near.

At the top of the second shoulder my heart's beating fast. Just as I find a spot to sit, a goanna suddenly flees up a ridiculously slight tree. We take in each others' presence before I sit. Feeling for it none of historian Manning Clark's 'eye of great pity', I call it a 'miserable sod'!

Next climb has a different reward. As we come around the bend there are familiar Mt Budawang, Currockbilly and the distant Budawang Range. Pidgeon House, so distinctively shaped, is also visible. So too is my old stamping ground of The Castle (or Cooyoyo) and the Monolith Valley complex.

And, to the west, the Corn Trail's two rounded mountains— formidable bulks, and all mine to climb. Between is the lower saddle, so, for once, we must descend (shown at 5 on the map). Guided by sight only, this time the early track makers had overshot the mark.

It has taken one and a half hours to reach the saddle. Ahead lie the steepest slopes where the Trail zigzags sharply upward. Only consistent pace and effort and a minute rest every five minutes sees me through. The reward is views towards both the Budawangs and the Buckenbowra River Valley.

Further up, the Buckenbowra's pastoral valley stands out, with the ocean horizon obscured only by the salty air. What grand sights each switchback offers!

On the way up it's apparent that the volunteers who rebuilt the track (as part of the Bicentennial) had to tackle a variety of dense vegetation types. Firstly 'The Knoll' (no. 6 on map), a silvertop ash forest subject to dense lower regrowth after severe bushfires. After passing along a ridge with fall-away slopes, further clusters of dense undergrowth are met—track makers cleared dense thickets of tristania on these upper slopes. Along the subsequent flat are thick stands of dry temperate rainforest species, especially sassafras. To re-establish the track these too had to be cleared.

The end of the walker's struggle is signalled at last by relatively flat terrain. There are two kilometres of smooth sailing ahead, with breaks recommended for the views or for a more detailed examination of the forest. Views to the coast and distant Pigeon House are possible when dense mist doesn't blanket the scene. Even then—especially then—standing amongst the mountain grey gums, the peppermints and bloodwoods is not a solitary experience. At any moment some strange, beautiful or unknown experience or thought could come into your life.

Perhaps your interest will turn to the small and intimate detail of the forest. Will you notice the stone cairn where the Trail meets the old cart track? Will you notice the rapid change of scene as you re-enter sandstone country? You will see grass trees (*Xanthorrhoea australis*), coral heath (*Epacris microphylla*), the common hairpin banksia (*Banksia spinulosa*) and the less common *Banksia canei*. Or perhaps, on reaching the wagon track, you'll just grin with satisfaction, and hurry along the last kilometre to a waiting vehicle or friends.

Whatever your experience it may be with both relief and regret that the old wheel ruts are followed. Will you prance along the last kilometre to the Corn Trail's end? I did, wondering whether this two wheel track was as old as the Corn Trail itself. There is supposed to have been a staging area here, as once the climb was completed the colonials would reload their produce and carry it on wagons.

From both an historical and personal view the walk is an enchanting one, and how close we feel to the early track makers' task. The track making problems and solutions are seen in the raw.

But were these problems solved 'by sight' as much as by 'inside knowledge'? During reconstruction work it was discovered that excavated sections had been superseded by later cuttings; another example of the 'hit or miss' of early track making? It should be remembered too that colonisers—the invading Europeans—were never safe from the (rightly) outraged indigenous people. Was this a factor in routing the track through relatively open terrain?

For myself the walk exercised both body and imagination, and was well worth the energy and perseverance required. I was moved to look over local maps, finding colonial names like Quart Pot Road, in the Bolero Valley. These names are widespread but their colonial meanings are fast fading. The Corn Trail is a physical reminder of tougher, more optimistic times.

Murramarang National Park

Fresh air, turbulent seas, warm sandy soils, forests of spotted gum, dappled sunlight and coastal rock shelves; we are enjoying the delights of coastal walking in Murramarang National Park. Situated 280 km south of Sydney, and 90 km east of Canberra, Murramarang attracts coast-loving Australians in good numbers during the summer and holiday periods, falling back into slumber during winter. With numerous small fringe settlements and caravan parks it is a relatively unspoilt space with more than enough natural attractions.

Murramarang is small—a mere 1600 hectares. Formerly a narrow section of state forest it was wrenched from the Forestry Commission in 1973. It is not as yet a marine park.

Murramarang NP is 27 km long and stretches from Murramarang Point to North Head (see regional map). However it rarely exceeds one km in depth. Embracing the beaches, headlands and easterly slopes of a small coastal range it also includes four islands: Wasp, Grasshopper, Dawsons and O'Hara.

The Settlements

The nearby settlements are integral to the park. From north to south they are Kioloa, Merry and Pretty Beaches (all in close proximity), Pebbly Beach, Depot Bay, and North and South Durras. Amongst them Pebbly and Depot beaches are the result of early forestry activities. North and South Durras, with Pretty and Merry Beaches to the north, were largely created by holiday-makers and local occupation by fishermen.

The settlements are a reminders of coastal villages in the 1940s and '50s, with a lone general store, simple tarred roads (usually only the main street), minimal

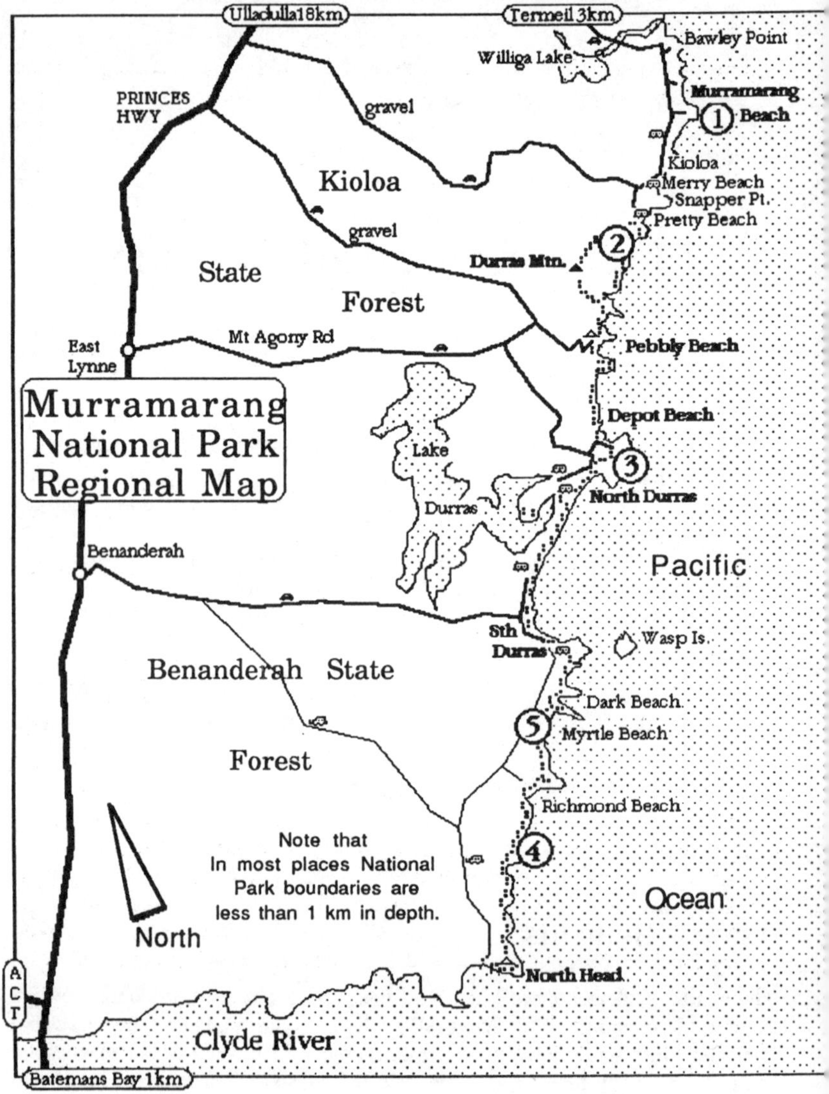
Ulladulla 18km
Termeil 3km
Bawley Point
Williga Lake
PRINCES HWY
gravel
Murramarang Beach
1
Kioloa
Merry Beach
Snapper Pt.
Pretty Beach
Kioloa
gravel
2
Durras Mtn.
State
Forest
Mt Agony Rd
East Lynne
Pebbly Beach
Murramarang National Park Regional Map
Depot Beach
Lake
3
North Durras
Durras
Benanderah
Pacific
Sth Durras
Wasp Is.
Benanderah State
Dark Beach
5
Myrtle Beach
Forest
Richmond Beach
Note that In most places National Park boundaries are less than 1 km in depth.
4
Ocean
North
North Head
A C T
Clyde River
Batemans Bay 1km

concrete, no curb and guttering (a dubious piece of progress) and a generally relaxed atmosphere. Typically people roam around in thongs, sandals or barefoot.

In fact the region is reminiscent of Vance Palmer's mini-classic *The Passage*. This 1930 story centres on a settlement around 'the passage' and the effect of modern influences on a small, isolated community.

When the story opens, the town has just become accessible by road. The central character, Lew, sees a beautiful stranger on the beach. The allure of the new is there but, as the story unfolds, we learn that everything comes at a price.

Like the settlement in *The Passage*, Murramarang's early European settlement centred on the cutting and shipping of timber. As roads to Sydney were unreliable, outgoing timber and incoming supplies arrived by ship. Nearby and regional forests around the Clyde River Valley had extensive supplies of timber, so that coastal settlements included sawmills, port facilities and schools.

Later, vehicular roads brought traffic—and holidayers to the South Coast. From the postwar period weekenders, cars and caravan parks confirmed a small, but crucial tourism industry. The cottages built were usually timber or fibro two bedroom houses, simple and undistinguished. Native and introduced grasses grew casually and unobtrusively around verandahs, and often to the road's edge. Fencing was an unnecessary ornament. While the buildings never had aesthetic value (some were downright ugly), careless, casual and haphazard elements created a admirable blend with the grassy surrounds.

Weekenders without fences are surely preferable to the ever-increasing fencing of property. Such fenced-in buildings are a heavy presence in any holiday spot. Minimal or no fencing is one factor that distinguishes these settlements from suburbia.

In fact the old village atmosphere is fast disappearing. Canberran affluence, suburban reproductions (called housing developments) and the real estate world's versions of progress have been mushrooming.

Modern affluence has not brought aesthetic wisdom. People are creating bigger, more intrusive, houses on the natural landscape. Sometimes their every element clashes with the surroundings, perfect reminders of 'conspicuous consumption'. Gardens were once as casual as the holiday-makers themselves—each having one or two native trees, a few geraniums in pots and shrubs for wind protection. Now they have neat rows of showy shrubs and annuals, cut lawns and manicured roses. Trees are stark, or gone.

Native vegetation is contoured by wind action and adapted to the coastal elements, whereas introduced species are usually conspicuous and inappropriate. The old-style gardens harmonised better with coastal conditions, and were certainly less work to maintain!

Access

Even today, travellers zooming down the highway are unlikely to casually visit the park. The minor spur roads leading to the park and its settlements are quite inconspicuous. Some forest roads are unsealed, most are partly sealed.

Access to Durras North, Depot Beach, Pebbly Beach and the northern section of the park is via the Mount Agony Forest Road from East Lynne, whilst access to the northern tip of the park is easiest from the Termeil turnoff for Bawley Point and Kioloa. (see Regional Map).

Accommodation

Every settlement offers accommodation, be it cabins, guesthouses, 'weekenders', campsites or caravans. Apart from Pebbly Beach, an exceptional niche, each have the usual public facilities of water, telephone, electricity, toilets, television and laundry.

Caravan parks are found in all the 'villages' except Depot Beach. There are at least six in all: two on South Durras, two on North Durras and, two in the north at Pretty and Merry Beach. Most maintain a very reasonable standard. All are well positioned and of appropriate pricing. Take your pick (try Batemans Bay Tourist Information).

Camping in the national park

Within Murramarang there is a brilliant array of attractive potential camp sites. But the NPWS rightly fears the consequences of numerous random sites. The coast has both a delicate ecology and a most compelling place in Australian culture. The combination only works if it is carefully protected from overuse. So camping within the park is in only two official sites: Pebbly Beach and North Heads. Otherwise the general NPWS rule is that bush camping is only permitted 100 metres away from any road, walking track or parking area.

Applying this rule to Murramarang is somewhat ironic as no such place exists!

Strangely enough, overnight bush camping in a nearby state forest site is allowed. Here the rules on camping are more permissive. Because Murramarang is so narrow you have only little distance to travel. And your site may be very attractive indeed.

Activities

Coastal parks such as Murramarang allow swimming, diving, surfing, beach games, relaxing, beach and rock fishing, photography and nature study. How about 'kangaroo-watching'? Roos are a common local feature—they're everywhere. Usually in small groups, lounging in the shade or on the beach, waiting expectantly between caravans, or just chewing on the lawn. No need for mowers here.

Ecology

The park's vegetation is dominated by tall stands of wet eucalypt forest. Pure stands of spotted gum with a burrawang palm understorey are common, particularly in the southern part of the park. Some isolated and sheltered gullies have small rainforest remnants, notably in the vicinity of Durras Mountain. There are also mixed forest communities and woodland which tend to occur in patches close to headlands, giving way on windswept headlands and beaches to heath, banksias and she-oaks.

The amount of animal life is comparable with any other area along the coast. Kangaroos and wallabies are particularly common and many other mammals may also be seen. Birds recorded in the park include parrots, honeyeaters, finches, thrushes, fantails and wrens as well as muttonbirds, albatrosses, terns, gannets, oystercatchers and members of the eagle and hawk groups.

Other features of Murramarang National Park include the many fascinating shell animals to be seen in rock pools along the seashore and significant deposits of Aboriginal relics, such as kitchen middens, which visitors are reminded not to disturb or remove.

Durras Lake is also of interest. It has been formed by the drowning of the eastern edge of the Murramarang Range which runs north-south hard against the coastline. A rare example of a coastal lake unscathed by urban development, it is now threatened by just such an event.

The best way to appreciate Murramarang's complex coastline is by walking. This way we can experience the headlands, cliffs, beaches, small offshore stacks, wave cut platforms and tombolas.

Our 14 walks cover the entire park, starting from Murramarang Point in the north, and finishing at North Head in the south.

Murramarang Point (Map 1)

Walk 1: Murramarang Point (Allow 2 hrs)

Murramarang Point is a small, separate section of the park. Easy access is gained by going to Gannets Beach settlement.

From an urban setting, walk along Murramarang Beach. Behind, and to the centre, of Murramarang Beach is a large scattered midden, with various-hued stone flakes and rocks scattered amongst the crustacean shells. The rocks (where did they come from?) were used to break open the food. Archaeological analysis has also discovered the bones of mutton birds.

Eastern Australia has the richest food stocks, so Aborigines lived here in great numbers.

The Point is historically important. Here, large groups of Aborigines gathered when James Cook's *Endeavour* passed. Carrying weapons, they gesticulated in hostile manner. Local elders have said the gathering was of approximately 500 people. Their version has been passed down to them, generation to generation. Cook also recorded the event.

Behind the beach is a freshwater lagoon, set amongst casuarina groves. This is largely private property, home to cows on pastures that must be marginal indeed. Sandhill embankments are set further towards the point, and, for a thorough walk, it is recommended to continue along the southern rock shelves. An access track for beach-goers leads to a parking area. (see Map 1).

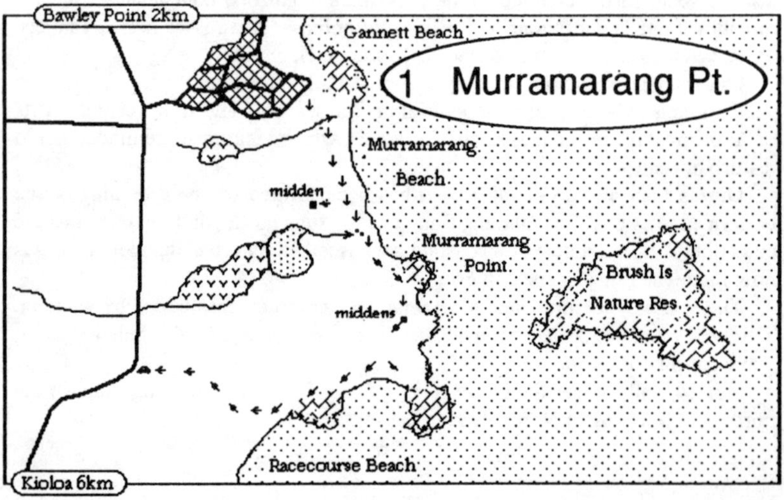

Durras Mountain Area (Map 2)

Walk 2: Pretty Beach and Snapper Point (Allow 1 hr)

Further south is Pretty Beach, a village of mixed fortunes. Nearby is a pleasant walk through banksia woodland to Snapper Point headland. The old vehicle tracks to the Point are often badly eroded, a consequence of the past vehicle usage. Still, the headland has been wisely preserved from development (unlike Bondi and Coogee). Its relatively small area provides aesthetic and recreational relief for locals who this walk of 400-500 metres. It is brief, but invigorating.

Snapper Point itself has outcrops of fossil-bearing rocks. This particular evidence of time past has scientific importance and receives special NPWS management. Snapper Point's plant communities feature low-growing trees and shrubs such as she-oaks (*Casuarina distyla*), swamp oaks (*Casuarina glauca*), geebungs (*Persoonia* spp.), rusty petals (*Lasiopetalum ferrugineum*) and the coastal rosemary (*Westringia fruticosa*). Allow time to enjoy the heath flowers, at their best from July to October.

Passing near the southern cliff faces there are panoramic views of the park including Durras Mountain, Depot Beach, Clear Point and nearby Pretty Beach. Look for the dense closed forest and dark green pockets of rainforest along the coastline.

Walk 3: Pretty Beach to Durras Mountain (Allow 4 hrs, return)

The Durras Mountain track is a pleasant open walk along (mainly) forest track. A distance of five kilometres, it has some steep uphill sections, exceptional amongst Murramarang walks. As the land has been cleared for past grazing the panoramic views are marvellous. On a clear day the Snowy Mountains have been sighted. More than likely you'll see the expanse of the Clyde River Valley. Behind it is the Budawang Range, with Pigeon House to the north. Progressing westward is a line of prominent features: The Castle, Mt Owen, Mt Corang, Admiration Point, Currockobilly, Mt Budawang and Clyde Mountain. To the south and north is the glorious coastline with its sandy and shingle beaches, rugged headlands, tombolas, rockstacks and fossil bearing rock. It's a joy to be here.

This coastline and its hills are geographically young, with much of the Budawang Range and surrounding valleys the result of advancing and retreating coastlines. As a barrier these hills are small, with Durras, at 285 m ASL the highest point. From here the western slopes fall slowly to the Clyde River. On the ocean side this narrow strip to the shoreline encapsulates Murramarang's spirit.

There was once a homestead poised on these hills, centre of small cattle property, now long gone. I have been told that this property was donated to the

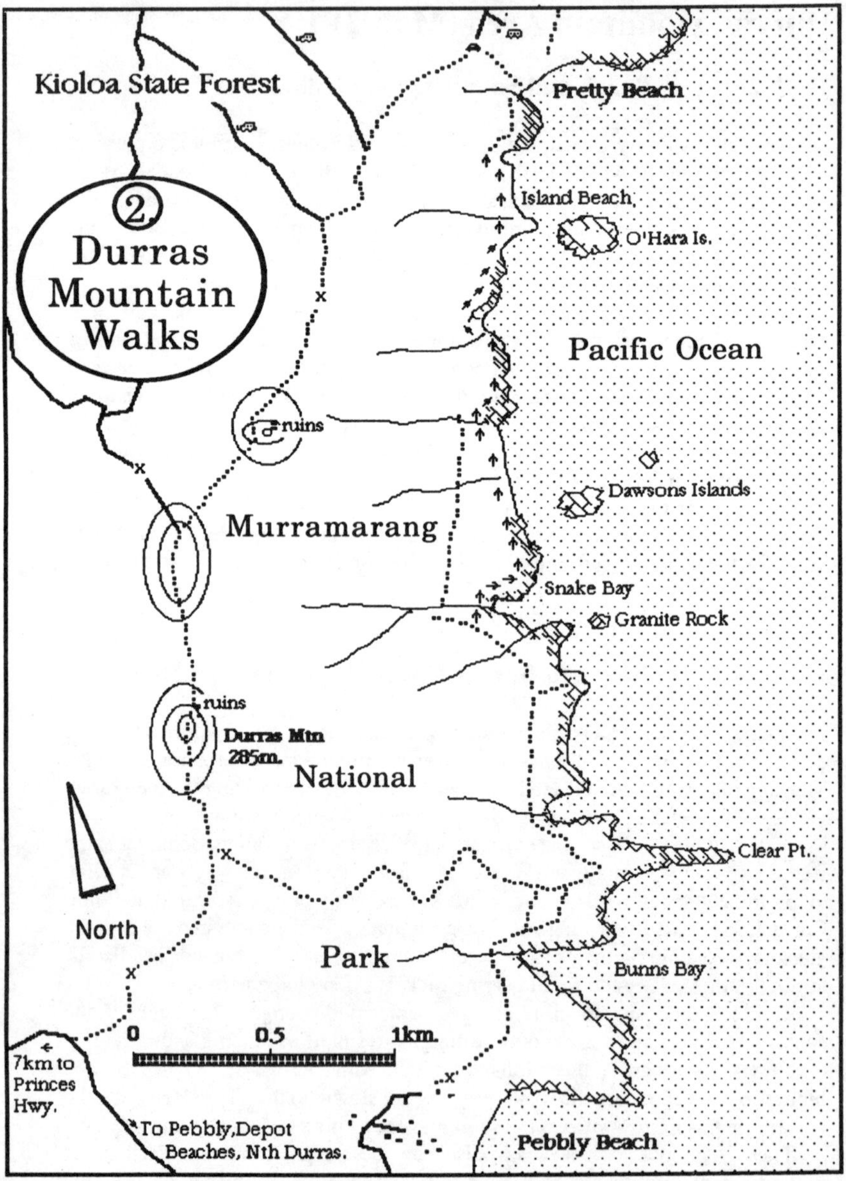
Kioloa State Forest
Pretty Beach
Island Beach
O'Hara Is.
2.
Durras Mountain Walks
Pacific Ocean
ruins
Dawsons Islands
Murramarang
Snake Bay
Granite Rock
ruins
Durras Mtn
285m.
National
Clear Pt.
North
Park
Bunns Bay
0
0.5
1km.
7km to Princes Hwy.
To Pebbly, Depot Beaches, Nth Durras.
Pebbly Beach

park. The homestead ruins, fruit trees and gardens are extant, and well worth examining.

For Aborigines, Murramarang has great significance. The Wandandians placed their dead in rock shelves under the Mountain, in a sense 'under' its care. Naturally there are legends and dreamings associated with the site. Rumour has it that with ongoing forestry activity a paternal religious minister exhumed the bones in case of forestry interference.

Walk 4: Durras Mountain, Clear Point to Pretty Beach
(Allow 3-4 hrs)

In the protected gullies below Durras Mountain are rainforest environs. Growing here is lilly-pilly (*Acmena smithii*), black wattle (*Callicoma serratifolia*), cabbage tree palm (*Livistona australia*) and bleeding heart (*Omalanthus populifolius*).

The walk down from Durras is a transition from pastures to open eucalypt forest, then to rainforest and finally to the open coastal grassy land of Clear Point. The track winds down steadily as it was once a forest access track to Pebbly Beach.

A walker making a quiet entry to Clear Point will typically find wallabies grazing here. Eastern grey kangaroos, swamp wallabies and an occasional red-necked wallaby can often be seen at dawn and dusk when they feed. Eastern grey kangaroos particularly, have become tolerant of humans due to years of care and patience from residents of nearby villages. Nocturnal animals such as possums, fruit bats and sugar gliders also live in the nearby dense gullies and open forests.

The variety of habitats here accommodates a variety of birds. Parrots and finches in the forest and forest edge, honeyeaters attracted to the flowering shrubs, and a number of seabirds, all inhabit the park. Sea eagles, black cockatoos and parrots may also be seen.

This coast is a delightful experience as it allows a combination of forest track and accessible beach walks. Walking along track from Clear Point to Snake Bay is one such stroll. Look out for a side track through dense heathland leading to the coastline. It's probably used by fishing enthusiasts.

The track appears to end at Snake Bay, so most people return to Pebbly Beach. However there are, in fact, two options for further progress: either follow the shoreline, or find another forest track opposite the creek. The coastal rocks are the best option, though if high tide cuts off access, the other is not too difficult to locate.

From the coast Dawsons Island is clearly seen, though the surrounding rock shelves and beaches are likely to steal your interest. Here are places of solitude and objects of curiosity. An example is two ocean chasms where waves storm into them, creating wonderful sound effects. The rounded stones are tossed wildly by water. Each chasm is only a half to one metre in width, so they are easily crossed.

A small beach is traversed to a headland. It is impossible to pass around its cliffline, so a scramble up a creek bed, then to the slope above lands us, surprisingly, on a track! Progress from here is easy, with a long beach and sandy spread ahead.

Central Murramarang (Map 3)

Walk 5: Pebbly Beach (1 hr)

Pebbly Beach is a special environment. Once a forestry village, much of it was leased from the Forestry Commission after WWII. The long term leaseholders have constructed well-spaced cottages behind the beach, creating a genuine village atmosphere.

The beach and much of the surrounds are part of the park. Exploring the beach area you may spot a timber post. Timber was punted or winched from here to steamers moored in the bay. A horse-drawn railway ran to the mill. Remnants of this track can still be seen at the back of the beach.

Also on the northern headland are fossilised worm burrows. They appear on the cliff face about one metre up. Look for dark grey traces up to 10 cm long and 1 cm wide. They are usually either vertical or oblique to the rock layers.

Further around the headland some caves are accessible around low tide. If you look inside you'll see thin horizontal layers on the rock face, remnants of when the land here was a mud flat in a shallow sea.

Behind the cottages is a public camp site. The ranger collects camping fees daily during peak holiday times. No bookings are taken, so no place can be guaranteed here. Nearby is burrawang forest on one side, and a stream on the other, home to rainforest species. Both areas allow short rambles into the gully.

Walk 6: Pebbly to Clear Point (Allow 2 hrs return, 1 hr walking)

Leaving behind Pebbly Beach we pass a locked gate, and immediately enter open forest with a burrawang understorey. Over the hill we see Bunns Bay. It might well have been better named 'Pebbly Beach' for Pebbly is actually a sandy beach whereas Bunns is rocky! The bay is always turbulent, which prevents sand from being deposited there. Nevertheless you'll be rewarded for lingering on its rocky shelves. Here are numerous rock pools, the life forms in each determined by the depth of water at low and high tide.

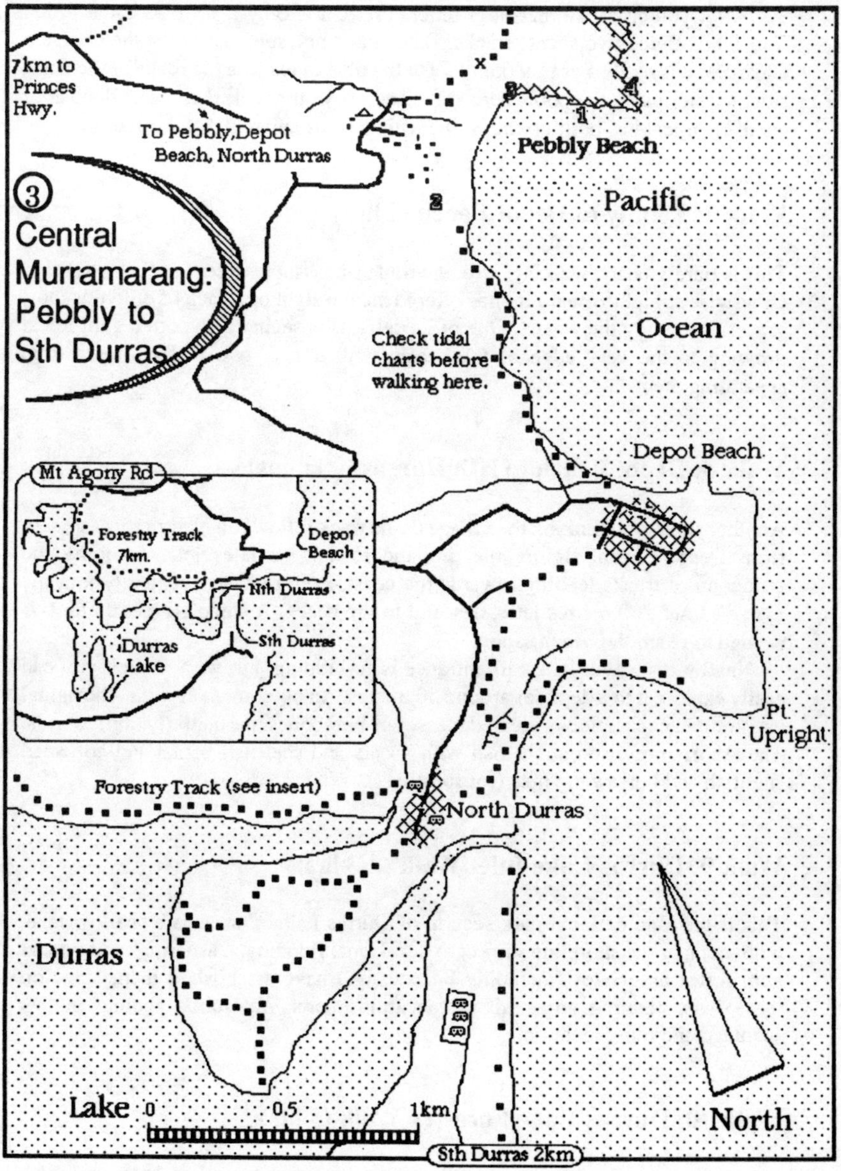

7km to Princes Hwy.
To Pebbly, Depot Beach, North Durras
③
Central Murramarang: Pebbly to Sth Durras
1
2
3
4
Pebbly Beach
Pacific
Ocean
Check tidal charts before walking here.
Depot Beach
Mt Agony Rd
Forestry Track 7km.
Depot Beach
Nth Durras
Sth Durras
Durras Lake
Pt Upright
Forestry Track (see insert)
North Durras
Durras
Lake
0
0.5
1km
North
Sth Durras 2km

After you cross another intermittent creek it is only a stroll to Clear Point. You'll be offered two access tracks. Take either, and soon marvel at the brisk air. Clear Point is really a grassy point! Take the time to explore the rocks of the north side. Mysteriously the pools here are raised above the rock shelves. A deposit of some chemical has built up the walls, with curious and delightful effect.

Walk 7: Pebbly to Depot Beach (1 hr+)

This is purely beach walking, with the route impassable except at 'lowish' tides. Otherwise straightforward it once offered me the sight of a pack of dolphins most gracefully plying the waters. One of its delights is seeing the spotted gum forest growing to the very edge of the beach, with only a two to five metre drop separating them.

Walk 8: Depot Beach to Nth Durras (90 mins)

Another short walk linking the villages. The track follows an electricity easement from Depot Beach. Before meeting the road it deviates left. Avoiding the seduction of tracks leading towards the coast, keep right to eventually join the road. A brief 200 metres later, descend to the beach. A steep 10 metre climb is needed to reach the beach sands.

Nearby is a cave. Its small entrance is forbidding, but with a torch you can easily explore it to a depth of around 50 metres. An obvious shelter for Aboriginal use, limited excavations revealed masses of bird bones, particularly muttonbirds. The Aborigines also caught fish with spears and shellfish hooks and collected shellfish and burrawang nuts (for roasting?).

Walk 9: Durras Lake Inlet Walk (2-3 hrs)

This is the lone national park section of Durras Lake. Durras is a shallow lake, with much of the shoreline subject to occasional flooding. Casuarinas and typical gum forest associates (including burrawangs) have established themselves on these flats, creating an unmistakable atmosphere. Waterbirds abound in this secluded and quiet location.

Walk 10: Durras Lake Forestry Walk (3 hrs)

For a longer walk, this time not circular, a forestry track has been included. Following almost seven kilometres of foreshore, this is a rare and pleasant walk through unblemished and peaceful environs. At one point the track passes over a rise through eucalypt forest with a grassy, sometimes tangled, understorey. Here I've seen many inconspicuous but beautiful fringed lilies (*Thysanotus tuberous*) set amongst native grasses.

For access from North Durras you'll need to ask for permission to pass through a caravan park. This is common courtesy, with permission (in my experience) always granted. An approach from the Mt Agony end makes things a little more difficult.

Walk 11: North to South Durras

Beagle Bay's long beach is best appreciated when it is walked. But first, the lake's entrance must be crossed. Usually it's closed, but when it's open I would not try it if there's an outflow. This could prove fatal, or at least far more dangerous than anticipated. If the crossing is possible, faster access to South Durras or North Durras can be achieved by walking behind the beach. There you'll find a convenient road, the caravan park access road.

Southern Murramarang (Maps 4 and 5)

These walks are in what is arguably Murramarang's most remote section, admittedly still laced with forestry road, but far removed from the madding crowd. Even so, short walks from a number of parking areas to nearby beaches are convenient for everyone.

With many possible short walks fairly apparent I've opted to describe three: from Richmond Beach to North Head; from Emily Miller Beach (near South Durras) to Richmond Beach; and one particular stroll around North Head. These walks can be combined into one circular walk.

The route shown in Maps 4 and 5 link forestry tracks, fisherman's and beach access tracks with some untracked terrain through spotted gum forest and coastal woodland.

Despite a lack of proper tracking there is little problem with accessibility. Walkers should, however, avoid damaging the forest, its vegetation and themselves.

The region's nomenclature appears contradictory: 'South' Durras is at the region's northern end, while 'North' Head is the Park's most southern point! Both take their names in relation to other places. North Head is the Clyde River's northern headland and South Durras is the southern reach of Durras Lake.

For access to North Head turn off the highway at Benandarah for South Durras. Turn right after 2.3 km onto a forestry road. However I do not recommend undertaking this venture by 'ordinary' vehicle; I've seen some troubled vehicle owners attempting retreat after a rainy night—not a pretty sight. This plight is avoided if the car is left at either Richmond or Myrtle Beaches. These are approached from South Durras.

The tall spotted gum (*Eucalyptus maculata*) with an understorey of burrawang (*Macrozamia communis*) is the dominant plant community of the park. The forest association runs the length of the park. Other forest species such as the blackbutt (*E. pilularis*), grey ironbark (*E. paniculata*), and bangalay (*E. botryoides*) do appear, especially where the forest grades into open woodland closer to the coast.

Walk 12: North Head (Allow 1-2 hrs)

The park has much evidence of Aboriginal occupation, but no part more so than North Head. Records to date show over 20 sites in the park, with North Head having one of the most interesting: a mine site.

We are outside the Sydney sandstone region here. The schists and other volcanic rocks are harder and more resilient. Here the rock has an added quality: it breaks up in sharp cleavage, yielding ready-made stone for Aboriginal implements.

A trade route probably started from here. These rocks would have been in demand in the sandstone regions to the north. Certainly a known trade route existed to the north-west, going up the Clyde and Yadboro Rivers and passing across the upper Shoalhaven; easy access to the north (more detail is given in Chapter 4, Budawang Magic).

Would this site have had a semi-permanent population? Certainly seafood was abundant, both fish and shellfish. The nearby lagoon would have been a source of permanent water. Study of the site, and its accompanying midden, indicates a long period of Aboriginal occupation, estimated to be for at least 1500 years.

European presence, though short, has had a more marked effect, with numerous old tracks noticeable. One leads from the beach up to the trig on the headland. Here only the sturdiest coastal species survive, with the spotted gum becoming lower-growing as you move up the rise.

The sand dune and midden there were being destroyed by the combined effects of wind, pedestrian traffic and vehicles driving on the beach. Restoration work involving the reshaping and grassing of the dunes is in progress. A walkway between a low fenced area has been built for beach access.

Apart from a walk to the headland the lagoon is worth a visit, if only for the opportunity to experience an undisturbed freshwater lagoon—there aren't many of these left on the NSW coastline. Surrounded by casuarina forest and a brush cherry understorey, it is a rare dip back in time. Quietly observe the bird and insect

Emily Miller 3km
4
rough
Benandarah
4wd
P
ruin
Richmond Beach
State
7
Murramarang
Southern
Marramarang
rocky
pinnacles
4wd
end
Little Oaky Beach
Forest
Oaky Beach
Pacific
National
Honeysuckle Beach
Park
North
41m
Ocean
0
0.5
1km
North Head

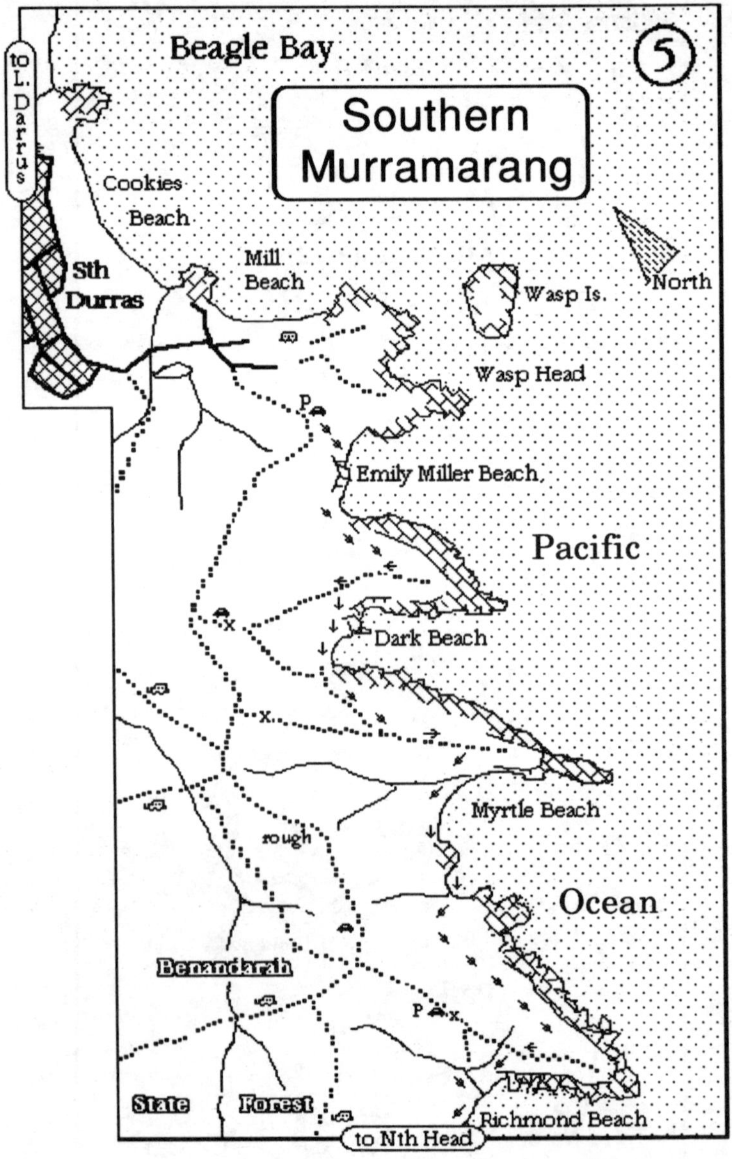
5
Southern
Murramarang
Beagle Bay
to L. Darrus
Cookies Beach
Sth Durras
Mill Beach
Wasp Is.
North
Wasp Head
P
Emily Miller Beach
Pacific
x
Dark Beach
x
Myrtle Beach
rough
Ocean
Benandarah
P
x
State Forest
Richmond Beach
to Nth Head

life on show; a wallaby may wander down for a drink—or a reptile.

Take a stroll to North Head itself; there are the inevitable, and delightful views to the south: the Clyde River harbour, with distant views of Batemans Bay and its satellite settlements. The Tollway Islands opposite are nature reserves.

Behind the beach is an official campsite, one of only two in the park. It has toilets and rubbish bins only. Take your own water. Note that the nearest town water is at Batemans Bay. Hopefully no vehicle access will be allowed in future.

Walk 13: Richmond Beach to North Head (Allow 3-4 hrs, one-way)

From a convenient parking area above Richmond Beach it is a short walk down to the beach. However a walk to the headland first takes you through typical spotted gum and burrawang forest, but as you advance to the headland, there is a progressive change. The height of the gums (which include ironbarks and stringybarks) is limited by exposure to the salty ocean winds. Note the small track heading towards the northern beach head. This leads to a ruin. What a position it once had, with grand views of Richmond Beach and the rugged southern coastline.

After Richmond Beach there is a long, trackless bushland section. Some four gullies (including the first at the beach's south end) must be crossed before the next forest track is reached. Though the vegetation behind high cliffs is often dense, prickly heaths, a little manoeuvring will keep you consistently within spotted gum forest.

This strategy offers a number of advantages. You'll notice the consistently sandy soils the forest grows on, leaving you wondering at their adaptiveness. You'll enjoy the dappled sunlight that passes through the trees; you'll learn quickly to weave a path through burrawangs which will leave you (hopefully) unscathed.

You may discover more about the ecology of the area, more of the spotted gum and the burrawangs. The spotted gum (*Eucalyptus maculata*), for example, is one of the region's most important hardwoods. As it is unsuitable for forestry harvesting the shortened and twisted forms have been spared to delight us. This gum occurs in coastal areas north from Bega, its mottled, pitted bark and usually straight bole are easily distinguished.

Commonly associated with them are the burrawangs (*Macrozamia communis*). These belong to an ancient plant group known as cycads. Burrawangs occur on sandy or stony soils. They are slow growing, averaging one new frond per year. The palmlike fronds arch outwards from ground level or from a short trunk. The male and female pineapple-like cones are borne on separate plants. The large yellow to red seeds have a high starch content and were eaten by the Aborigines after vigorous washing to remove toxins.

The simple combination of burrawang and spotted gums produces more botanic and visual variations than might be expected. A few other species are always found, sometimes in strange liaison with the dominant species. For visuals the sight of the forest overlapping with the beach and ocean is beautiful and relaxing.

Just before the fourth gully there is an optional descent to Little Oaky Beach. Here is a view of the spectacular rock strata between Little Oaky and Oaky Beaches. Massive beds of sedimentary rock have been uplifted, folded and eroded, leaving enormous sculpted walls.

Leaving Little Oaky Beach, cross more open forest to the ridge top. Here you'll meet a track. Either use the two tracks to reach the beach, or take the shorter, overland route. This route should put you above the beach for a fine view. More interesting however is the quite bizarre example of stunted spotted gum found there. So exposed is it on the cliff top that its branches have grown horizontally, and the 'trunk' looks like a pincushion.

The beach is then reached by passing westward through a teatree glade. Eventually you'll reach the track that leads to the beach sands.

Another exploration is to pass around the coastline south of Oaky. Eventually you'll go no further, but the trip is worthwhile.

Oaky to Honeysuckle Beach is a choice between track or untracked walking. If you've just completed the earlier section, the tracked walk may be more enjoyable. From there to North Head is adequately shown in the accompanying map.

Walk 14: South Durras to Richmond Beach (Allow 3 hrs, one-way)

South Durras to Richmond is another fine Murramarang walk, with the return walk quite direct. Otherwise you may be tempted to continue to North Head. Use your imagination—you could arrange a pick up and return to Batemans Bay in time for a seafood dinner.

Your best starting point is Emily Miller Beach, with perhaps a preliminary stroll to Wasp Head. Around its rock platform are uncovered fossil beds, an old boiler (a remnant of sawmilling operations) and scenic coastal views.

Emily Miller Beach is followed to its southern end. Enter the forest, and walk uphill keeping close to the coastline. At the hilltop you'll meet a vehicular track, which can be followed back a little way, or simply ignored and crossed.

Once you have made your way across to the southern side, explore the cliffline area. The rock shelves below appear to open a route to the beach, but are best avoided. Keep to the bush and slowly make your way down.

Before doing so, notice how the beach is divided by a rugged rock outcrop. On one side the beach is shingled and grey; on the other, conventional and sandy. We are at Dark Beach, and this features the junction of the most southern point of the Sydney Basin sandstone. Around it are intensely folded chert and pyrite metamorphic rocks.

From just above Dark Beach it is a simply a matter of joining a track to the south. Follow it out to its end. Here is a truly grand Murramarang vista with panoramic views north to Grasshopper Island and south as far as the eye can see. Just off the headland is Flat Rock Island.

Myrtle Beach is particularly attractive with its broad sweep and varied depth. The transition from sandy beach to rainforest occurs over 100 metres.

After the main section of the beach follow around the rocky outcrop. Here you'll find some amazing examples of folded strata in the inter-tidal zone. The resulting erosion has left a extremely rugged surface, almost impossible to walk on barefooted. One section was so like a crocodile's back that I called it the 'crocodile rock'!

After this there is a 500 metre section of spotted gum forest and burrawangs. Make your way up carefully. For best results, don't rush. Richmond Beach is not far ahead. If you've enjoyed it so far, how about continuing onwards to North Head?

A Murramarang Trek

For a two- to three-day coastal trek Murramarang offers a unique combination of attractive features and convenient touches of civilisation. Starting from the Kioloa area (either Murramarang or Pretty Beach) go to North Head and—damn it—arrange for a beach pick up to Batemans Bay. Snapper for dinner!

Camping or other accommodation can be organised. Do it which ever way you like.

Murramarang's Future

Murramarang is a young national park. It appears to be almost unchanged from the former forestry years. Everywhere there are forest roads, a higgledy piggledy array of tracks to headlands and beaches which are unrelated to national park objectives. Are all these tracks needed? Where should there be better access, and where more restricted access? Should longer walks be accommodated by additional tracks, or encouraged to use more coastal access? These are questions relating to what can only be called our 'natural heritage'.

The park is only a small part of a much larger region, where urban and recreational pressures will increase in future. What is to happen here? How much, and what type of coastal development should be allowed? With population build up (I believe) inevitable, what type of development will accommodate a quality of life in harmony with the surroundings and how should this be encouraged? How can all the relevant authorities come to agreement over such a process?

These are long-term question which must be considered. Otherwise the warm sands, the shingle beaches, twisted rock strata, the Aboriginal heritage and beautiful forests could be part of a coastal city stretching from Cairns to Melbourne, an urbanised, over-commercialised nightmare. Rather than see this happen, I'll place myself under the care of Durras Mountain and all its ghosts!

Budawang Magic

Standing before the Seven Gods Pinnacles we look at the proud sandstone edifices protecting this ancient city of nature. The curved walls and cascading layers are eroded beneath to caverns. Each pinnacle's form is unique.

By walking alongside these guardians the bushwalker can gain admittance to Monolith Valley's inner sanctum. You pass through a narrow stone gateway framed by ancient fig roots, scramble down the ziggurat-like ramparts, and are finally initiated into Budawang Magic.

The Budawangs—as the area is fondly called—is a high plateau, the most easterly part of the Southern Highlands. Cut off by the turbulent northward push of the Shoalhaven River, to the east its landscape boldly drops away to within only 15 kilometres of the Pacific Ocean.

From the top of the plateau are clear views of the ocean, yet coastal visitors barely notice the range. Some holiday-makers might venture to picnic at, or climb, Pigeon House, the one isolated and distinctly conic Budawang peak. Rarely, though, do they enter the surrounding forests or mountains further inland.

At the heart of the range is the unique and enchanting Monolith Valley, a Budawang high watershed housing rainforest pockets, heathland, woodland and sedgeland. Each is tightly distributed around small sandy streams and rocky slopes. Mountain run-off feeds the plant life.

The gullies, submerged streams and natural arch never fail to appeal, whether to naturalist or artist. The mighty sandstone mountains of Donjon, Owen, Cole, Shrouded Gods, Nibelung and the Seven Gods Pinnacles are eroded forms that define the valley. The brilliant array of sandstone forms fire the imagination, suggesting lost Aztec cities or sci-fi images of strange, fantastic planets.

Monolith Valley resembles a classic European castle. It is defined by its high position over the Clyde River and Yadboro valleys. The mountainsides form the castle walls; the mountain tops are the castle's towers and parapets.

Of these, rugged Donjon—the word itself a castle feature—overlooks Holland Gorge to the north; the massive Shrouded Gods surveys Pigeon House Gorge and the Upper Clyde River to the east and north; and mysterious Nibelung and Owen feed the Yadboro River. Only from the west is there a drawbridge entry—across a grand saddle joining Bibbenluke to Mt Cole's stony face (see map). This is more than enough to draw a party of walkers into adventure.

On this particular walk we aimed for the saddle entrance, starting our trek from northerly Newhaven Gap. Normally this takes two days, with a third allowed for the descent to Yadboro. We allowed four, aiming to enter Monolith Valley on the third day, and leaving the fourth for the difficult descent.

The Journey Begins

We start at Sassafras, a lofty former volcano with 1600 hectares of rich basaltic soils (potato-growing country).

Sassafras is an hour's drive south-west of Nowra. Blink and you'll miss it: there's no main street, nor shop; only pastures and a few ramshackle sheds. There are glimpses of the distant Pacific Ocean.

A farm gate takes us onto a minor track which passes over private land. This is our access to the southernmost regions of Morton National Park. By tradition, permission is not required—only the courtesy of closing gates and respecting farm property.

Ordinary cars can take the track in dry weather; but in wet weather the track is definitely not recommended.

Our destination is Newhaven Gap, a narrow way between two ravines. During the 8 km drive the basalt soils disappear, replaced by arid sandstone terrain with mallee gums, tea tree (*Leptospermum* spp.) and wattles (*Acacia* spp.). The many gates and bumpy ground makes progress slow.

Oddly shaped outcrops, wind eroded and craggy, dot the landscape. To the east unlikely hints of grandeur: a giant north-south crack in the land—the first jagged cuts made by the Clyde River headwaters. To the west another cut, this one east-west. We're riding the high saddle between the Clyde and Shoalhaven Rivers.

At Newhaven Gap we leave our transport in a small bushland parking lot. We'll see it again on the fourth day.

The walk's first five kilometres passes through a quirky landscape pitted with small gullies and featuring eroded sandstone outcrops. We meet no one. A light wind gusts around us. The weather is overcast and the even light makes it hard to determine which way the creeks are flowing. It's eerie.

Then—a sudden change in the landscape: rich volcanic soils with dense stands of tall sassafras and tangled, barbed vines occupy the rise. At a T-junction, beautiful stands of tall stringybark and white ash shade a grassy understorey. This is The Vines.

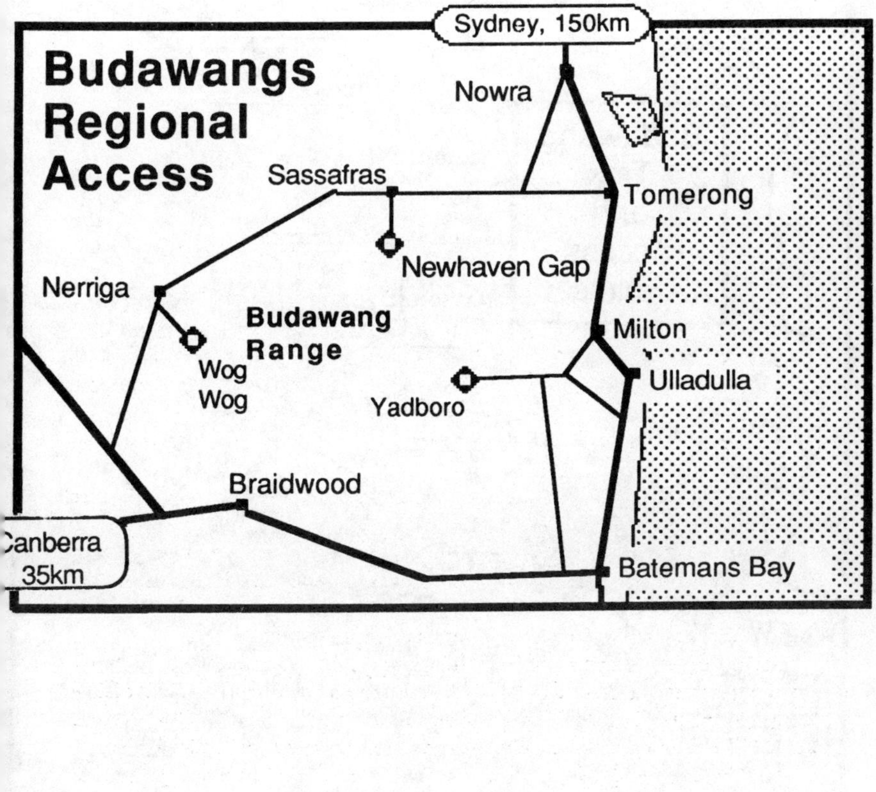
Budawangs Regional Access
Sydney, 150km
Nowra
Sassafras
Tomerong
Newhaven Gap
Nerriga
Budawang Range
Wog Wog
Milton
Ulladulla
Yadboro
Braidwood
Canberra 35km
Batemans Bay

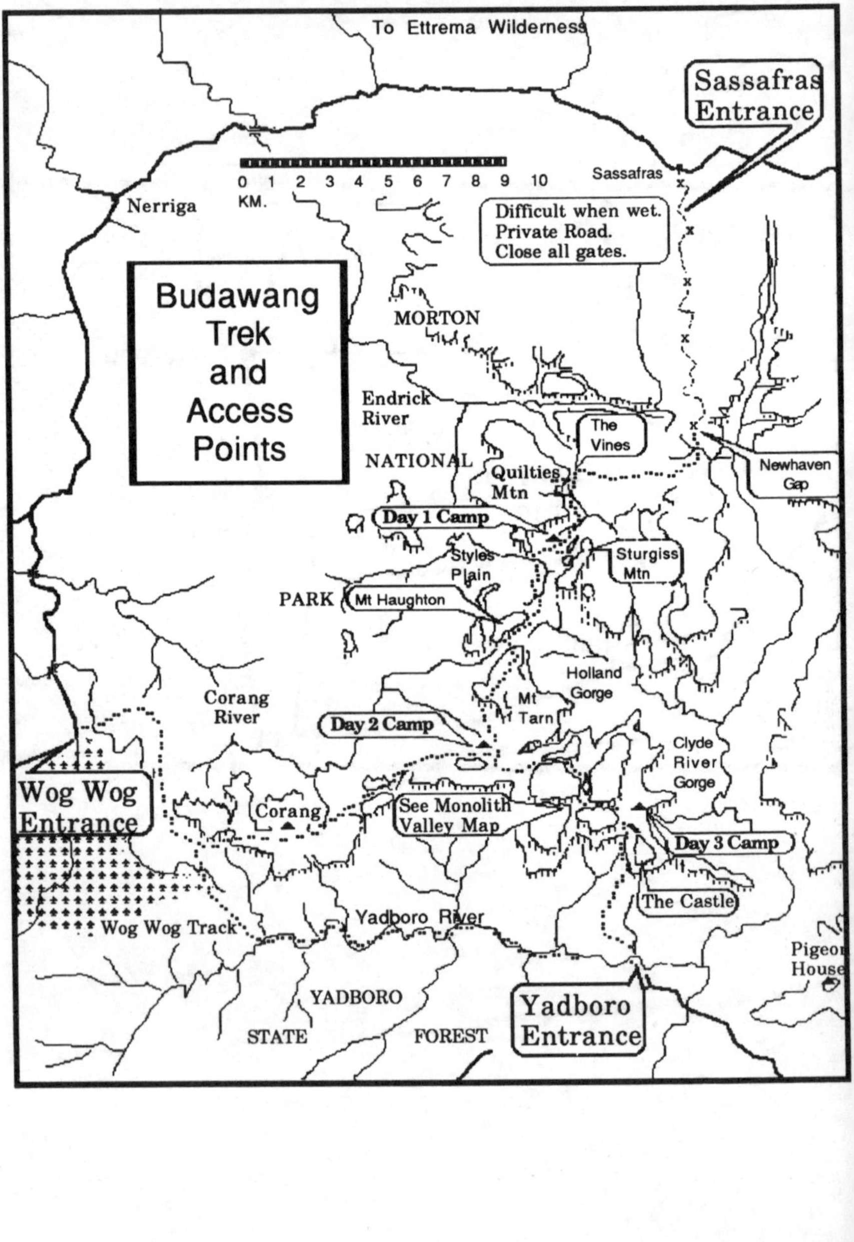
To Ettrema Wilderness
Sassafras Entrance
Sassafras
0 1 2 3 4 5 6 7 8 9 10
KM.
Nerriga
Difficult when wet.
Private Road.
Close all gates.
Budawang
Trek
and
Access
Points
MORTON
Endrick
River
NATIONAL
PARK
The
Vines
Newhaven
Gap
Quilties
Mtn
Day 1 Camp
Styles
Plain
Sturgiss
Mtn
Mt Haughton
Holland
Gorge
Corang
River
Mt
Tarn
Day 2 Camp
Clyde
River
Gorge
Wog Wog
Entrance
Corang
See Monolith
Valley Map
Day 3 Camp
The Castle
Wog Wog Track
Yadboro River
Pigeon
House
YADBORO
STATE
FOREST
Yadboro
Entrance

In the 1840s the old Wool Track, carrying wool from the Monaro to coastal shipping, ran near here. The White Cat timber mill operated here from the 1920s until 1933, when it was destroyed by fire. During the 1890s depression, subsistence farming and small-scale cattle grazing flourished here.

A mysterious Bill Styles lived in a hideout below, near Quilties Mountain. One Mark Piercy eked out a living as a potato farmer and the Quilties brothers constructed a pass on to Quilties Mountain, allowing cattle access to its (very) limited pastures. Others ran cattle along an Aboriginal trade route between Wog Wog and Sassafras—even grazing, it is claimed, on remote Mt Tarn.

The Bora Ring

Once The Vines is reached, an Aboriginal Bora Ring is close at hand. We reach this magnificent arrangement of stones with an 80-metre climb up cascades of sandstone. It is a large oval stone arrangement, eight metres long and bisected by a straight line of stones. Nearby is another arrangement: a heavy, elongated, erect stone about one metre high, held by a mass of smaller rocks. Slightly further away are scatters of rocks, some may have also have been man-made, but their form is now all but lost. Amazingly the ground was only officially recorded in 1932.

The Ring is high on this isolated mountain, away from hunting grounds, clearly separated from the plains. The location marks it for sacred ritual status and use, perhaps including a taboo to those of another sex or 'skin'.

The Bora Ring's exact ceremonial purpose can only be a matter of speculation. The rapid and devastating European occupation destroyed local Aboriginal culture—the new occupants took little interest, and showed scant respect. However the shapes suggest the male and female sex organs; and it is surely not coincidence that Pigeon House itself is unmistakably like the female breast and nipple.

The Way Ahead

Having seen the Bora Ring the return walk is doubly rewarding, taking us to a splendid panorama. From the left—northward—is the track from Newhaven Gap. In front is the Kilpatrick Creek Gorge which later flows into Holland Creek

Gorge. To its left is Island Mountain, a trackless section of plateau abruptly ending at the gorge. The outer section looks like lawn but in fact is low heath growing off a sandstone base. A sharply defined central area is eucalypt woodland, just as exposed as the heath but built on a poor quartzite base.

To the right is Sturgiss Mountain, holding within it Hidden Valley, a popular destination for bushwalkers. If we swing further right—to the south—we see Pagoda Rocks and the southern tip of Quilties Mountain. Between is open forest on a large rise, our first night's camp. Beyond is Sallee Plain, Mt Haughton, Hoddles Mountain, Mt Tarn, and beyond that, the saddle to Monolith Valley.

This expansive setting is the essence of the Budawangs: grandeur, variety and wildness. Its various communities are all before us: closed and open forest, woodland, heathland, sedgeland and rainforest. They hold a total of 700 species. Many are common to other sandstone districts, but some are endemic to the region, including Pigeon House ash, (*Eucalyptus triflora*), and Braidwood waratah (*Telopea mongaensis*). At least 16 species are listed as rare or endangered.

On the larger canvas, the neatly defined plant communities of the Budawangs are visually outstanding, almost diagrammatic sketches defining complex geological histories, natural adversities and (comparatively) recent landscape developments. The plunging cliff lines, mesa-like mountains and evocative sandstone forms make this a wondrous scene.

We can also see the route ahead. Below are the headwaters of Kilpatrick Creek. Our path, an abandoned forestry track, passes through an extensive rainforest gully. Using logs to cross the last stream we will climb a hill between Sturgiss and Quilties Mountains.

We are looking at a piece of bushwalking history here. This route is closely linked with earlier attempts to climb The Castle, just beyond Monolith Valley. On the Anzac Weekend of 1955, for example, a Sydney Bushwalkers party first attacked the Budawangs by crossing Kilpatrick Creek rather than taking the longer route over Quilties. However they crossed further downstream, missing the easier forestry track we follow. Their route forced them to climb into Hidden Valley, later exiting onto Sallee Plain; a direct but extremely difficult assault. In the limited time available to them, the 1955 party only managed to reach the southern summit of Mt Tarn.

Our group easily reaches its prearranged destination, camping atop the rise between Quilties and Sturgiss. Here is a heavenly, peaceful site: an open eucalypt forest, the floor matted with native violets, numerous grasses and a sprinkling of graceful and decorative tree ferns, home to wombats, cuckoos and fruit bats. Above is the twinkle of stars between curved branches and hazy foliage.

Styles Plain

Next day we take a side journey to Hidden Valley, an enclosed marshy valley on the eastern edge of Sturgiss Mountain. At one end of this mountain breach is a sweeping view of the second day's walk. From the right we can see the edge of the open forest where we camped; then the sudden transition to Styles Plains; and, in the distance, the base of Mt Haughton. That afternoon we would follow Mt Haughton's cliffbase to far Mt Tarn, camping (beyond our line of vision) on the headwaters of the Corang River.

Later in the morning we reach Styles Creek on Sallee Plain. Pungent heaths and herbs in the dwarf scrubland communities are an immediate delight to the senses. Most are neatly rounded by wind action. The scaly trunks are bizarrely bent and twisted. On the ground lichen, moss and smaller herbs survive in shallow, rocky soil and thin litter. Only a few mallees poke their heads above one metre, their thin, flexible branches surviving battering winds from both ocean and mountain. Here and there are patches of flowering grasses, lilies, melaleuca and lomandra.

At last we turn off the old forest track to a welcome padded route. We enter wilderness. It baptises us with light rain. Curling mists rises out of Holland Gorge, and Styles Creek's thoroughly soaking sedgeland is underfoot.

Our party is surprised to be walking knee deep in water, with uneven tussocky sedge making balance precarious, and non-tussocked heaths above limiting vision. Indeed the way the track breaks up along the wetland edges shows where others have attempted to avoid it. Too bad! The sedgeland is best crossed directly and with little fuss.

Once across we are very close to the edge of Holland Gorge, the 400-metre-deep giant cauldron which is eating away at Sallee Plain. As it is obscured by mist, we continue along the steep neck of Mt Haughton. The day is bizarrely calm, the light even, giving a kind of incandescence to the forest foliage

Reaching the cliff base we walk southward, surrounded by the sounds of falling water, as temporary cascades fall gurgling, crashing and rushing over every cliff and crevasse. The lush and drenched foliage droops across our route. We are soon very wet. Within fifteen minutes I know we won't cross Mt Tarn today.

At the base of all the Budawang mountains are sandstone overhangs. It was in one of the larger and deeper overhangs that we make camp. Although we are a little disappointed at falling short of the saddle, pushing on could have proved disastrous. The mist is thick, the rain light yet constant. A soaked party of walkers would be tempting fortune to follow the obscure track across Mt Tarn.

Crossing Mt Tarn

On the third day the weather clears, but not before we cross Mt Tarn—at a moderate 900 metres ASL, the highest point of the walk. Although now well fed, dry and in good spirits (despite the weather being at this stage little better then yesterday), we are however behind schedule and must make Monolith Valley today, or the last day will be rushed and so become dangerous.

As it happens, crossing Mt Tarn is both an anxious and beautiful affair. An early start sees continuing light rain, like a veil of mist. With some foreboding we cross the saddle joining Mt Tarn to Haughton, then thread our way between the rocky outcrops. On top the heath is all-pervasive, a grey-brown dotted with cream tea tree flowers. There is nothing else to be seen except mist.

The way ahead lies in finding the track through the heath. The track is not always apparent as it easily becomes overgrown, but having found it we move on. Ghostly rock outcrops appear beside us. Normally these outcrops can be climbed for breathtaking views of Holland Gorge, but not today. The bare rocks are like sculptures. Wet, with a dullish gloss, they are weird, sometimes malevolent forms.

A quick rest gives us time to relax, remove rucksacks and appreciate the silence.

For once Mt Tarn cannot offer its usual sights—even Anvil Rock on the Tarn's south-eastern corner is blanketed by mist. The small pool too has disappeared beneath surrounding heath. Although the rain has subsided somewhat, the windless day means that the mist persists. Soon we are all keen to move on.

If we had known what lay ahead we would not have been so keen. Here, at the highest point of the walk, our next obstacle is a swamp swelled by rain. My fellow walkers need some persuasion to walk though it, boots and all.

With the rain persisting we trudge through the swampy grass and heaths. As we are moving towards what should be Anvil Rock the track breaks up into small pads, so we again cross swamp, only to find ourselves back where we started.

There is nothing for it but to cross the swamp a third time (I, most apologetic!) and we are faced with a choice of three or four other tracks. I now take the best—and the least wet—track for our fourth crossing!

We plod on. The trick from here is to avoid descending the first two narrow ravines. Both spell trouble; both must be crossed. Only the third ravine gets you off Mt Tarn, with a remarkably simple and short descent.

There is another aspect to the wildness of Mt Tarn. According to Wilf Hilder (in *Pigeon House and Beyond*, pp. 37-38), the Hollands built a cattle yard there in the 1890s—an amazing claim for two reasons: the vegetation seems like poor fodder, and access is difficult even for walkers. The question is, how did they get there?

Only one approach—the one we took across the saddle—is feasible. But a different route would have been needed. A track would have been required. The

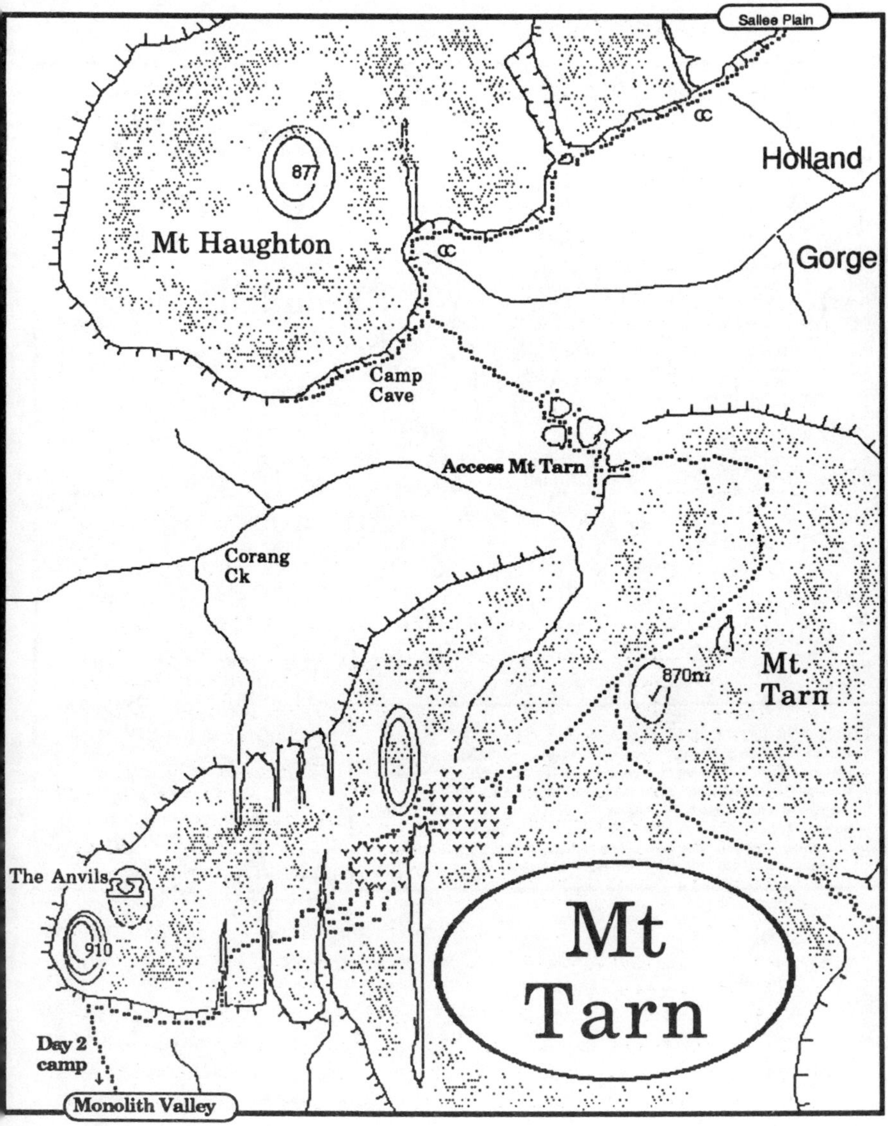
Sallee Plain
Holland
Gorge
877
Mt Haughton
Camp
Cave
Access Mt Tarn
Corang
Ck
870m
Mt.
Tarn
The Anvils
910
Mt
Tarn
Day 2
camp
Monolith Valley

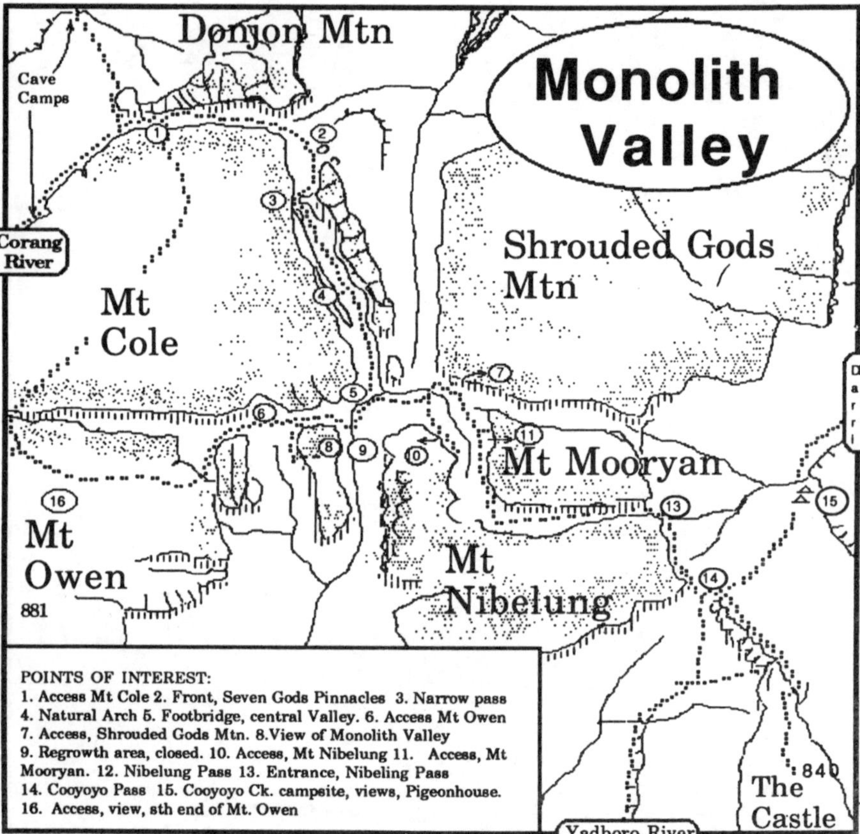
Donjon Mtn
Monolith Valley
Cave Camps
Corang River
Shrouded Gods Mtn
Mt Cole
Mt Owen
881
Mt Mooryan
Mt Nibelung
840
The Castle
Yadboro River
POINTS OF INTEREST:
1. Access Mt Cole 2. Front, Seven Gods Pinnacles 3. Narrow pass
4. Natural Arch 5. Footbridge, central Valley. 6. Access Mt Owen
7. Access, Shrouded Gods Mtn. 8.View of Monolith Valley
9. Regrowth area, closed. 10. Access, Mt Nibelung 11. Access, Mt Mooryan. 12. Nibelung Pass 13. Entrance, Nibeling Pass
14. Cooyoyo Pass 15. Cooyoyo Ck. campsite, views, Pigeonhouse.
16. Access, view, sth end of Mt. Owen

answer lies in Hilder's earlier and more substantiated claim: that two Aboriginal tracks have long been used by Europeans as bridle tracks, one joining the Corang region to Sassafras. This would have brought the track some two kilometres west of Tarn. If a link track were made along the base of the southern faces of Hoddle and Haughton, it would have been possible to drive cattle along it. But the mystery remains: did it happen this way? Certainly finding the phantom stockyard would be a start.

Monolith Valley

As midday approaches we push on. The sun makes a fighting reappearance; Monolith Valley beckons. The enchanting forest slopes and rock overhangs of Mt Tarn have to be passed without full appreciation. Soon we are all struck by the sudden appearance of open heath and grassland, with the mighty bulks of Mt Owen, Mt Cole and Donjon at last in full view. Everyone stops; the sun beams down on both us and the great walls. Veils of mist rise slowly before us. Donjon's jagged peaks appear all the more magical, their black and sandy-yellow cliffs glistening with rainwater.

Bushwalkers Jack Cole and Tom Owen would have seen a similar sight in 1938, during their attempt to reach and climb The Castle/Cooyoyo. It was not easy. They reached the gully separating the two sandstone mountains, later named Donjon and Cole. From here they scaled Mt Cole, their progress stopped by the crevasse separating Cole from the southerly Mt Owen. The Castle, still distant, was to remain unclimbed for another ten years. Monolith Valley's treasures were not documented until Alex Colley's visit in November 1957.

It takes us just an hour to reach the point where Jack Cole and Tom Owen diverted upwards to Mt Cole. Here at the entrance to Monolith Valley we meet a NPWS sign, the first we've seen since the walk's start. It reads:

> Monolith Valley is an upland watershed with a series of valleys radiating from a central area of heath and woodlands.
> Cool temperate rainforest occupies these moist valleys and includes the plumwood tree, *Eucryphia moorei*, a remnant of Australia's cooler and moister past.
> Trampled vegetation and compaction of often saturated soils is causing severe erosion. Please help regeneration of this unique area by keeping to the designated walking tracks.

To enter the valley we descend briefly into an enchanting narrow glen. Often in shadow, Donjon's southern wall has been undercut by a stream. The air is always cool; rainforest remnants, mosses and ancient root systems conjure up tales of fantasy. Part of the track is within the creek bed, then it rises onto a series of sandstone platforms. Emerging into stronger light we move abruptly from wet, tree fern environs to dry heath—precious survivors growing on Mt Cole's thin, sandy soils.

The dense heath continues for some distance before opening to the first of the Seven Gods Pinnacles. This is an isolated, sculptured, sandstone knob. Approaching it, our attention is diverted to the magnificent view of Holland Gorge, a deep plunge of space between Donjon and Shrouded Gods Mountain. Then the multiplicity of forms of Donjon catches your eye, and the first of the Seven Gods is obviously related to them. This profusion of textures, spaces and forms leaves us speechless—the mind is simply unable to rapidly encompass it.

Given time we all settle down and enjoy the views, taking in each gem separately.

Shrouded Gods is worth inspecting. A careful climb up the first pinnacle gives a splendid panorama. The strange forms of the Seven Gods Pinnacles can be seen. The lava-like walls of Mt Cole conjure images of crowded Roman amphitheatres, the audience steeply banked over the spectacle of battles and bloodthirsty acts. Whether Hollywood-addled or European influenced, the imagination may unashamedly indulge itself here.

It is time to move again—we have yet to enter the valley's inner sanctum, and we must be out of Monolith before nightfall. We parade past each citadel, occasionally dipping into a dry creek bed. To the right a small gully reveals an underground cave. In it are insects unknown to me, One, holding onto the roof of the cave, is anaemic and long-legged; a curious sight.

Climbing to a small peak, the track passes around a rockface and immediately passes through a ziggurat-like rampart. Here, the vegetation is covered in moss and lichen; elaborate roots clinging to the mossy, ferny cliff. A welcome bevy of light pink petals sprinkle the ground. Skirting around a rock outcrop we pass through a narrow stone gateway framed by ancient fig roots, a magical entry to the valley floor.

There is much more—from the larger features of the natural arch and the pagoda-like walls of Mt Nibelung, to the smaller, intimate ponds, underground streams, balanced rocks and green carpets of moss.

The forms, surfaces and spaces of the Budawangs, particularly of Monolith Valley, suggest fantastic metaphors. One person has commented 'Now that I've seen this I won't need to visit Borobodor'. He was talking of a high overview of the valley, taking in Nibelung's eroded western wall, compellingly like the 100 pagodas.

Observing the natural arch in the Valley's inner sanctum, another said 'It's like a giant lifesaver dropped from the sky!' and another: 'I think I've found the lost city of the Aztecs' (the ziggurat-like ramparts at the northern entrance are reminiscent of an Aztec city).

'Lunar' said another, referring to the high rocky grounds around Mt Mooryan and Nibelung.

Interestingly many of these references already exist in the valley's nomenclature: a donjon is the inner defensive tower of a European castle; Shrouded Gods is an Etruscan reference, and Nibelung and Seven Gods are from Wagner's 'Ring of the Neibulung', better known as 'The Ring Cycle'. (In 'The Ring Cycle', the Niebelung are a race of dwarfs.)

Paradoxically, we have imposed upon the wilderness names that go to the various roots of European culture. Yet we couldn't be further away. The naming is an attempt to pin down, to orientate, and tame a wild place.

Such names are interesting, but limiting—each of us is free to interpret the valley differently.

The valley is a magical place, and to visit it can be an uplifting, almost spiritual experience.

There's no easy path out. We must rise to a rocky shelf, the complexity of forms around us distracting and everywhere apparent. Behind us are Seven Gods Pinnacles, the bulk of Mt Owen, and narrow watershed gullies.

With the sun low in the western sky, the dome-like shapes of Shrouded Gods, Nibelung and Mooryan are a gallery of forms glowing in a strange light. Still we mustn't dawdle. Before us are rockshelves, the track disappearing behind heath, or petering out at stone walls.

Beneath our feet is shallow leaf litter and moss clinging to barely definable soil. The hardiest heath species survive more from run-off than from soil: by day coping with bright light (both direct and reflected); by night withstanding freezing valley air. Our stark, long gully is far removed from the moist environs below.

The Return

The climb out soon brings people back to earth. A steep, narrow easterly pass must be found before we can leave the gallery heights. A short drop into a dry creek gully must be scaled with chains. After a long haul down a narrow enclosed gully we finally emerge into the open. The walker again meets the moist, cool overhangs formed by an underground stream. Unknown to us we've been following its deep cut into the mountain's walls. Making our way along the cliff base brings us to the pass between Nibelung and The Castle.

We have traversed a great part of the Budawangs—from Newhaven Gap to the brutal bulk of The Castle.

Here, memories of my first walk in this area return. We were returning from Monolith Valley, stumbling through the heath and eucalypt woodland at Nibelung's base, when I experienced the shock of my life. This gigantic black thing leapt out of the bushes at me. In that moment I thought (ludicrously) 'leopard!', as its screech was fearsome and wholehearted. When the shock wave passed, I could see a large black bird with a full two metres wing span. It was a black cockatoo, full-grown, and caught feeding on the ground. It rose up, wings beating the air, wheeled around, flapped furiously and sailed through the gap between Mooryan and The Castle. I stood amazed, and gazed admiringly after it.

Later in the afternoon a westerly weather pattern moves in. From the overhang we watch a cloud bank pressing towards The Castle's walls. Smashing into them, the cloud is pushed skyward by tremendous air pressure. Then, like the action of a gigantic funnel, most of the cloud is sucked through the pass, the mallee bushes below turbulently sweeping this way and that. A loud sucking sound is heard. We watch the power of persistent air pressure from the shelter of our dry overhang. Nearby, water gushes over the cliffs of Mt Nibelung.

We make camp on Cooyoyo Creek ('Cooyoyo' is probably the Aboriginal name for The Castle; it should be used again).

Next morning a heavy mist settles in. The air is still, the water still falling. Only the sun's dim light provides a portent of change. By late morning the mist begins to rise, so we set out to climb The Castle for the first time. There is still hope of a grand view.

We first climb a pinnacle, part of the Castle's 'tail' (see map). Having passed the rising mist we come to a point between two pinnacles, before us is a 50-metre plunge. Standing there, all eyes look out; to my surprise I see absolutely nothing. Steadying myself on this precipice I look downward and receive a second surprise—I see a human figure with a rainbow around its head. The recognition is instantaneous: it is like the rainbow figure found in Aboriginal art. Where had I seen these? In an *Australian Encyclopaedia,* when I was aged nine! It is a spirit figure found in Wandjina paintings in the Kimberley region. Here was the same vision found as a natural phenomena: a shadow projected onto the mist, the distortion of light forming a rainbow. I felt privileged.

Now for the descent to Yadboro River. Having relaxed in the morning (much needed after our three solid days of walking) we are ready for the descent and exit. In sunny weather we climb 600 metres down through rugged terrain with full views of the expansive valley of the state forest. For the first time we can see westward beyond Mt Owen to Mt Corang and Admiration Point. Southward are the imposing Mt Budawang and Currockbilly.

Once below our rewards are a dip in Yadboro River and a fresh orange brought in by our bus. We have trekked the Budawangs!

For my part, visiting Monolith Valley and the Budawangs again had put me in touch with my imaginative self. Like any holiday, an environment providing relief from urban demands, family, job and the like, provides space for our 'other selves'. In the Budawangs, with their outstanding forms and spaces, I have found no finer place to discover these things. And I am not alone…

World Heritage Barrington Tops

It's an odd experience to put your head out at dawn and see 'nothing'. Well, almost nothing...just grassy tufts, forlorn and drooping with water, an outline of a ghostly tree and a solitary ashen fireplace. The sounds of thumping hooves had awoken me, but I could see nothing. The plain was shrouded in mist and light rain; the only sound was of dripping water, and there was a cold breeze. We were not in fog; we were in the clouds, at 1400 m above sea level, hidden under nature's frosty blanket.

Later that morning the sun miraculously reappeared and, after a day of downhill walking, our next camp was beside canopy rainforest. There amongst the antarctic beech and giant banksias, the cool dank air might have been locked in a safe, for outside it was relentlessly hot.

A short wander around this closed world was an uneasy experience; the forest floor is sparse, rocky and dark, a forbidding combination on sunny days. Nearby gushing mountain streams beckoned.

Around dusk, when all else was quiet, friendly, long-tailed mammals such as the bandicoot, possum and pademelon emerged. From the vines at the forest's edge on one night a possum performed for some food. Only slight encouragement was needed to draw it close to the fireplace. Its antics, charming and cheeky, entertained us for an hour.

To experience such contrasts is typical of the Barrington Tops region. Subalpine plateau, swamps and eucalypt forest occupy the Tops; while river basins, open forest, grasslands and subtropical rainforests have the slopes. In summer the farmland valleys sizzle in temperatures of up to 40 degrees Celsius, while on the Tops snowfalls have occurred within a few hours.

Its wildlife include survivors. The wombat is one of the few natives to make its permanent residence on top. Below, rare animals such as the Hastings River mouse and rufous scrub bird are found.

The Plateaux

The two linked plateaux of Barrington and Gloucester Tops are part of the Mt Royal Range, a southern offshoot of the Great Dividing Range. Surrounded on three sides by the Hunter region distant views of the Pacific Ocean, some 90 kilometres away, are possible. The highest point of the Tops, Polblue, is only a pimple on the landscape, but at 1576 m, easily dwarfs more famous Blue Mountains peaks.

Its height is based on the resilience of the basaltic and granitic rocks, formed by a volcanic eruption, and hard and tough enough to resist natural forces for 50 million years. While the Great Dividing Range is ancient, the uplift of the Tops in the Tertiary period may be seen as recent. While mountain streams slowly eroded the softer, underlying sediments, the upper levels remained, forming an increasingly sharply defined landscape. Today's steep and dramatic slopes—especially around the Devils Hole—are impressive.

The Ecological Divide

The Tops area is also an ecological divide: although mountainous, rainforested and subalpine on top, below is the Hunter Valley, a plain made up of open forest and (now) land cleared for agriculture. Such differences have caused many animals and plants to reach their geographical limit on Barrington's slopes and high tops. The Hastings River mouse, for example, is at its southern limit on the southern slopes of the Barrington Tops. The antarctic beech, the fragrant pepper bush, mountain walnut, prickly ash, rose maple, yellow carrabeen and thick-leafed laurel also reach their southern limit here. Still others reach their northern limit, including a number of ferns species, some primitive flowering plants of the Tasmannia genus and a number of orchids[1]. Barrington is another 'great divide'.

The Tops as Watershed

The Tops area is a regional watershed. Anyone standing in rainforest near the escarpment will recognise the 'squish' of soaked soil underfoot. Water oozes from all points, the result of obstruction by the Tops of major weather patterns. Small flows make their way down densely vegetated slopes, quickly becoming streams.

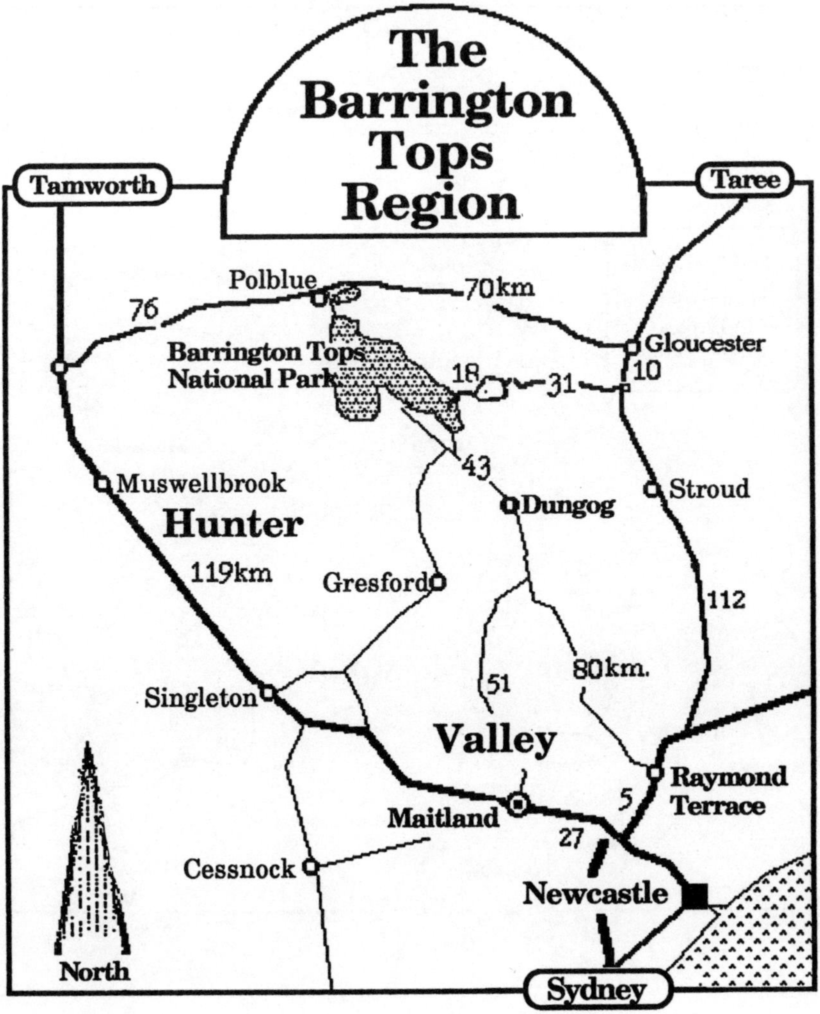
The Barrington Tops Region
Tamworth
Taree
Polblue
70km
76
Gloucester
Barrington Tops National Park
18
31
10
43
Muswellbrook
Stroud
Dungog
Hunter
119km
Gresford
112
80km.
51
Singleton
Valley
Raymond Terrace
5
Maitland
27
Cessnock
Newcastle
North
Sydney

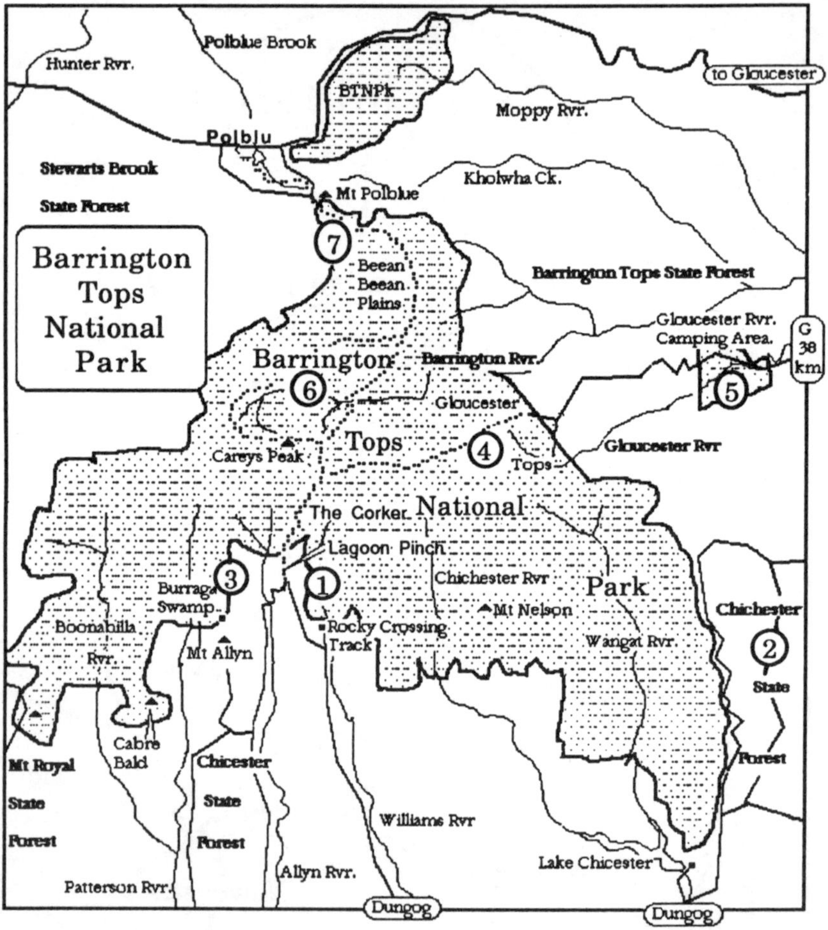
Barrington Tops National Park
Polblue Brook
Hunter Rvr.
BTNPk
to Gloucester
Moppy Rvr.
Polblu
Stewarts Brook State Forest
Kholwha Ck.
Mt Polblue
7
Beean Beean Plains
Barrington Tops State Forest
Gloucester Rvr. Camping Area.
G 38 km
Barrington
Barrington Rvr.
6
5
Gloucester
Tops
Careys Peak
4
Tops
Gloucester Rvr
The Corker
National
Lagoon Pinch
3
1
Burraga Swamp
Chichester Rvr
Park
Chichester
Mt Nelson
Boonabilla Rvr.
Rocky Crossing Track
Wangat Rvr.
2
Mt Allyn
State
Forest
Cabre Bald
Mt Royal State Forest
Chicester State Forest
Williams Rvr
Lake Chicester
Allyn Rvr.
Patterson Rvr.
Dungog
Dungog

From these come a range of rivers: the Patterson, Allyn, Wangat, Williams and Chichester in the south; the Hunter to the west[2]; and the Barrington and Gloucester (which both join the Manning River) to the east.

The southern mountain streams are major sources of the Hunter River, providing most of Newcastle and the Hunter Valley's water supply, via Chichester Dam (Wangat River) and others. For our purposes all these river sources are considered part of regional Barrington Tops.

The sphagnum moss swamps of the Tops are particularly important. These absorb large quantities of water during the wet periods, slowly releasing it over a long period. So the Tops area's water supply persists in the drier months, always releasing high quality water.

Aboriginal Occupation

For Aborigines the geographical barrier of the Tops acted as a territorial limit, with the Geawegal occupying the west, the Gaddhang in the south-east (Karuah/Myall/Port Stevens) and the Birpai to the north and east (Manning River/Taree).

Aboriginal tribes, divided into clans with distinctive names, routinely occupied particular areas of Barrington's slope and plateau.

A 1933 study shows that the Worimi tribe occupied country extending from the coast as far west as Barrington Tops, which 'according to the old residents, they visited in summer time'[3].

By the time Europeans began gathering information, as sketchy as it was, much of the remaining tribal kooris had been driven onto higher ground. European contact could be deadly. Historical material held by the Forestry Commission includes a matter of fact account of a European reprisal raid: 'The main body of Aborigines was camped on the north side of Mt McKenzie on Gloucester Tops on a narrow granite shelf above a cliff. Here they were surprised and all leapt to their death'.[4]

Evidence of Aboriginal occupation is still sketchy. A survey of usage of northern NSW rainforests found numerous artefact scatters adjacent to creeks. Sacred or other significant sites are fewer and most have been found in state forestry or on private properties. Within the national park no proper archaeological work has been carried out. From work completed at lower altitudes it appears that the ridges were used as pathways for travel to or over the Tops.

The Rainforests in Aboriginal Life

The cedar getters so efficiently felled lowland rainforests (below the national park) that it is today impossible to appreciate their original scale. All the surrounding farmland valleys were once lowland rainforest or open sclerophyll forest[5].

Today, most of the southern slopes rainforests are within state forest or national park, with most lowland flora and fauna found in these upper rainforests. The earlier preoccupation with the lowland's extensive resources kept loggers away from this upriver rainforest; later, better forestry management practices and national park status saved it from oblivion.

Denis Byrne points to an irony here: 'today's highland rainforests were almost unknown to these early Europeans, while the rainforests of the (Aboriginal) world are gone and unknown to us'.[6]

Rainforest provided a key habitat for Aborigines. It provided a great range of foods: animals like pademelon, flying fox, brush turkey, carpet pythons and other reptiles, birds and grubs; and vegetables in the form of seeds, fruits, roots and tubers. As well they made implements from certain vines, bark and leaves.

Perhaps the main rainforest food was the pademelon. Habitually solitary, its restriction to the fringes made it easy to catch. Although hunting individually was possible, collective hunting was the norm. Tribal hunting groups of up to 50 have been recorded in northern NSW rainforests. The common technique was to encircle and net the pademelons. Dingoes were used sometimes as well.

Flying foxes were knocked out of trees with clubs, speared in trees or caught on the ground after a tree had been felled. They were probably a feasting food, with records of groups of 100 or more Aborigines in the nearby Karuah Valley sitting around fires, roasting and eating them.[7]

Equally important was the gathering of vegetables like the cunjevoi and black bean seeds. To remove toxins, both were pounded, leached and cooked prior to consumption. The yam and other tubers are also found in these forests. One of the main foods would have been fruit, particularly the fig, which grew in abundance. With no preparation required it would have been an attractive 'off the tree' food.

As we stroll through these forests it is the vines and palms that immediately create our sense of 'jungle'. As a plentiful part of the Barrington lowlands they were an important source of a number of other products for the Aborigines. The bark from the giant stinging tree was fashioned into line and cord. From this they produced hunting and fishing nets and dilly bags. The pounded or chewed fibre was also used for soaking up honey as it was scooped from the hive. Vines were also used for tree climbing, as well as for lashing and shafting stone axes. Bangalow palm leaves were easily adapted as water carrying vessels.[8]

Recent research based on the southern state forests shows only three known sites of Aboriginal occupation, mainly within Chichester State Forest. This is a stark contract to the rich archaeology of the nearby Hunter Valley.

Other evidence suggests that Aborigines occupied the forest fringes, close to major food sources. Presumably camps were made nearby, but outside the dark, wet environs of the subtropical rainforest.

Dawson gave an intriguing 1830 account of the Gaddhang Aborigines of the Karuah Valley, an area partly within Chichester State Forest. He refers to smoke from grass fires 'in every quarter', later 'frequently ascending in thick clouds at a distance on all sides of us'.

Aboriginal fire practices were connected to their hunting and camping needs. Creating clearings within or on the rainforest fringes allowed more effective pademelon hunts, better organised camps and space for large ceremonial performances.

European Occupation

The minimal European occupation of the Tops is closely tied to development in the Hunter Valley[9]. Settlers first concentrated on the valley's rich alluvial soils. Some exploration of the Tops was undertaken but, due to the difficult terrain and climate, the area was largely neglected.

However settlers have long used the plateau for summer grazing, sometimes with disastrous results. In 1872, for example, 1100 head of cattle died there. The harsh lesson meant that only one permanent settlement—near Junction Pools—was erected. Grazing continued until 1969 when the park was established.

On Barrington's slopes it was a different story, with cedar getters and loggers gradually making inroads up the valleys and into the lower slopes. Goldmining and gem prospecting also occurred, with the Wangat goldmining village having a short lived existence. It is now in ruins.

By the turn of the century the area was recognised mainly for its hardwoods and several state forests were proclaimed. At the same time there was a surge of scientific interest. In 1914 the plants and animals of the region came under the scrutiny of Musgrave and Hedley of the Australian Museum. Other expeditions were undertaken by Professor Harrison of Sydney University, the Royal Ornithologists Union (1925), Dr Frazer and Ms Vickery (of the Benowie Track fame) and Musgrave again, several times (1944-48).

From the 1930s the Barrington area became a popular destination for tourists. The Barrington Guest House was built in 1930 to cater for packsaddle trips to Carey's Peak. Several planes crashed in the Tops. Although some have never been found, the remains of a World War II Mosquito bomber on 'Aeroplane Hill' (see p. 107) is a popular destination. I believe the propeller still hangs in Barrington House.

Conservation

Since the time of the Musgrave and Hedley expedition there has been growing support for the preservation of the region's flora, fauna and scenic riches.

Following World War One there was an increased feeling of national identity, and a corresbonding interest in all things uniquely Australian. Tourism flourished, and there was a new push to preserve the Barrington Tops region.

In 1924 a track that would take two weeks to walk was mapped out. In 1925 a Bird and Animal Sanctuary was established. In 1948 the Barrington Club was formed to popularise and promote the conservation of the area. There was a push to develop it as a Blue Mountains-style tourist destination for Newcastle and the Hunter Valley.

In 1959, after substantial lobbying by conservation groups, the Gloucester Tops State Park was proclaimed around Gloucester Falls.

In 1969 Barrington Tops National Park was created when the State Park was extended to the Barrington Plateau.

In the late 1970s there was a movement to protect NSW rainforests. After an inquiry the Wran Labour Government passed the 1984 Forestry Revocation and National Parks Reservation Act, resulting in major additions. The tiny Bird and Animal Sanctuary of 1925 now totalled almost 40 000 hectares, still only twice the size of Ku-ring-gai Chase National Park.

World Heritage Status

In the 1980s Barrington Tops National Park joined Kakadu, the Great Barrier Reef, Willandra Lakes, western Tasmania, Lord Howe Island and Uluru (Ayers Rock) as an Australian World Heritage area. Its large rainforest domains in the north-east, eastern and particularly in the southern sections are one of 15 rainforest areas known as the 'Subtropical and Temperate Rainforest Parks of Eastern Australia'.

Such recognition is two-edged: the park has been committed to World Heritage management standards. By the same token its recognition will increase public awareness and interest. The area's unique natural attributes increase its attractiveness as a recreational resource.

Accommodation

There are hotels, motels and caravan parks in nearby towns. The Barrington Guest House, adjacent to the Williams River Area, is closest to the park.

Camping: In the national park, car camping for normal vehicles is limited to numbered campsites in the Gloucester River camping area. No bookings are taken and no fees charged. In state forests, camping areas are extensive, but also packed in holiday periods.

Camp sites on Barrington Tops are available to four-wheel-drive vehicles only. You are welcome to backpack into any area of the park, as long as you camp more than 300 metres from the roads, walking tracks, formal camp sites and picnic areas. Naturally, vehicles must remain on the roads.

The Southern Slopes and Rainforests

Perhaps the most popular attraction of the region is the luxuriant subtropical rainforest, mostly found on the southern slopes (see maps 1, 2 and 3). In forestry jargon these are known as 'ribbon' forests, dominated by native crabapple, sassafras, corkwood and silver sycamore. Several rare species are also found in this, the most accessible part of the Tops.

I first visited here in 1970. Having motorcycled to the Allyn and Williams Rivers from Newcastle, where I was a student of the university, I was quickly seduced by this natural paradise.

Rainforests were utterly new to me, as were mountain streams. I had been brought up to expect Dorothea Mackellar's 'sunburnt country, a land of sweeping plains'. Large river boulders, coloured pebbles and gushing waters, and the forest's mosses, lichens, tall eucalypts, elaborate vines and impenetrable undergrowth were all part of a new sensual delight. Even after the long ride on a 90cc Honda, using every ounce of its dubious power, it still seemed more than worthwhile.

Being young, in love, and totally unprepared meant that forestry picnic tables were our 'tents'; our meals, pieces of fruit, cheese and plain bread.

Such youthful romanticism is not to be envied, for without proper preparation you may find your visit spoilt. Leeches are plentiful, especially after rain. They're highly attracted to warm blooded humans, and may approach from any angle. Some people swear that these 'wet ones' maliciously drop from high branches. When I once revealed this to a couple, they immediately retreated to civilisation!

Rainforests also have stinging plants, whether they be trees, bushes or vines. These are the visitor's second risk. Take the 'Stingos'.

More attractive are the antarctic beech forests. Beech, combined with prickly ash, sassafras and other associated subtropical rainforest species are found at 700 to 1000 metres ASL. These are commonly encountered on the southern slopes, including parts of Chichester State Forest.

The southern slopes and rainforests present great variations for walking. Apart from rainforest there are impressive eucalypt forests, grassy 'balds' and high swamps. Most walks are over short distances—the shortest is only a hundred metres or so. The notable exception, from the Williams River (440 m) to Careys Peak (1640 m), is one of Australia's toughest ascents.

For the surefooted, one way to enjoy local walking is over river rocks. This can be inspiring. Mountain rivers provide rare clearings within rainforest, giving ample light and a channel for water and air currents. Away from the usual walking tracks, and surrounded by the sounds, sights and aromas of the forest you are instantly transported away from civilisation. Here is a solitude pregnant with possibilities: a channel of large, crashing sounds that assault the ears as effectively as rock and roll, but predating it by at least ten thousand years.

The river is also a highway of life, with insects on the fringes, fish and yabbies in the water, animals drinking from the edges and birdlife flying down the aerial corridor. Solitude? Here is a place where the respectful visitor can imagine, reflect and observe with great reward.

Discovering a natural slippery dip (see the Rocky Crossing Walk), spotting a flock of sacred kingfishers playing in upper river reaches, or just seeing the multitude of waterlife—these are everyday events.

Try imagining yourself as hunter or gatherer occupying these environs; open all your senses to the earthy aromas, peppery and herbal smells of the forest trees, to the colours of the river waters and the sounds of flowing water and rainforest. Enjoy the full sensations of life itself.

The Rocky Crossing Walk

For a traditional walking track close to Barrington Guest House, start with the Rocky Crossing Track[10], found on Map 1. This track takes a gradual climb through serene and relaxing rainforest. Generally subtropical in form, it includes some interesting variations. Allow about three hours for the complete walk; or meander over shorter distances. Follow your curiosity, breathe deeply, perhaps bravely dip into the chilly river waters.

As you step into the forest, listen for a variety of bird calls. Listen keenly and see if you can identify some of the common calls. The yellow-tailed cockatoo, *Calyptorhynchus funereus*, has a rising and falling screech. The bell miner, *Manorina melanophrys*, sounds like a small bell, whilst the call of the eastern whip bird *Psophodes olivaceus* as the name implies, is like the crack of a stock whip. The superb lyrebird, *Menura novaehollandiae*, has its own distinctive calls,

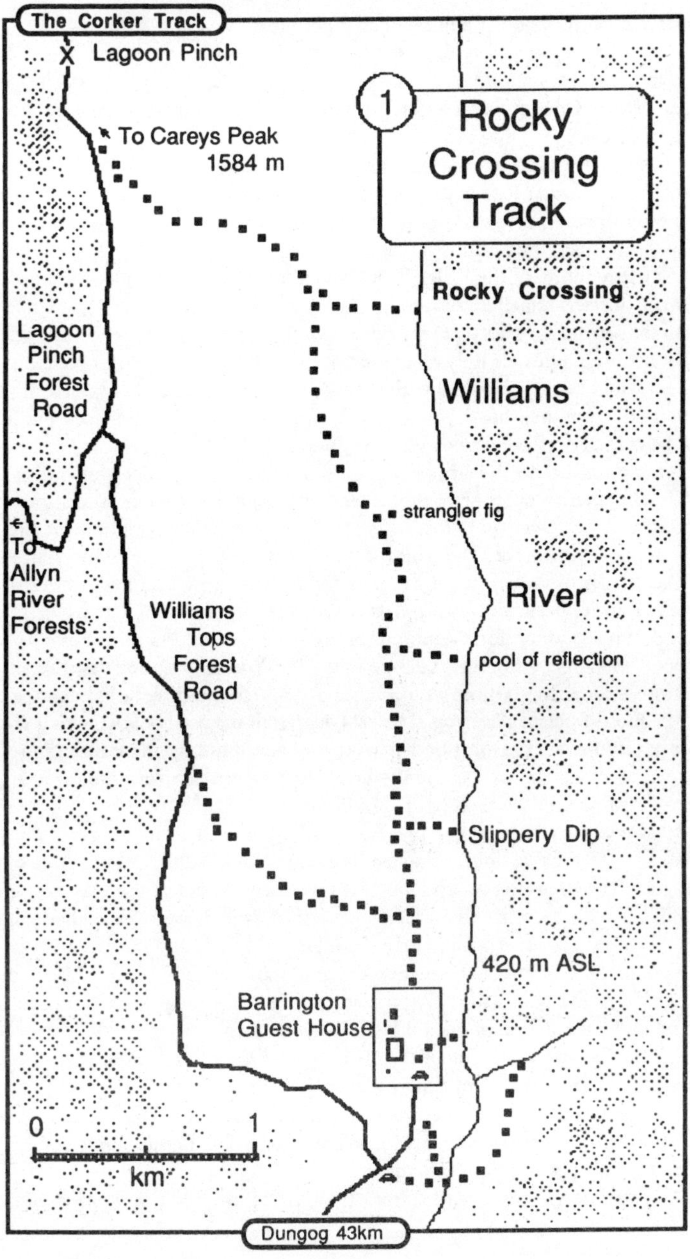
The Corker Track
Lagoon Pinch
To Careys Peak
1584 m
1
Rocky
Crossing
Track
Rocky Crossing
Lagoon
Pinch
Forest
Road
Williams
strangler fig
To
Allyn
River
Forests
Williams
Tops
Forest
Road
River
pool of reflection
Slippery Dip
420 m ASL
Barrington
Guest House
0
1
km
Dungog 43km

but is a great imitator of a number of other birds, so don't be fooled.

The sharp-eyed will realise that logging took place some time ago. A variety of rainforest trees including the red cedar (*Toona australis*) were taken from the forest, and the disturbance and regrowth have created interesting changes in the pattern of trees growing there.

Australian plants commonly have hard woody leaves (like the eucalypts) which inhibit water loss in drier climatic conditions. Not here. Most of the plants in the rainforest have soft, shiny leaves, indicating that there is usually moisture to spare in this humid atmosphere.

At the junction of the Ridge Track and a few metres beyond, you should see a number of ferns attached to trees. Look for the birds-nest ferns, *Asplenium nidus*, and elkhorn ferns, *Platycerium bifurcatum*, high in the trees. These ferns are known as epiphytes, as they attach themselves to trees but are not parasitic. They collect water running down the tree trunks and obtain nutrients by catching leaves which fall from their host. You may also find some epiphytic mosses and lichens. See how many different ones you can count.

At the turnoff to the Slippery Dip is a large Sydney blue gum (*Eucalyptus saligna*) standing taller than the other trees. Against it leans a forlorn looking turpentine tree, *Syncarpia glomulifera*. Look closely at the bark of these two trees; they are quite different. The fruit (or nuts) of the trees are quite different too.

At the Slippery Dip is an excellent spot for sliding and swimming. It is an exhilarating experience: position yourself, feel the force of the water pushing, look down the slope for orientation, pray—and let go! As you move down the Slippery Dip you will feel a change in the air. You may notice that the air is not so humid. Near the bottom you'll certainly notice the directional change of the slide. Oooh! Splash! And you'll be cast deep into the pool below, which is etched deeply into the rock. Don't bother worrying about hitting the bottom; you can't. As you come up for air, position yourself like a porpoise with the flow, and take a second slide into the next pool. Thrilling!

Between the Slippery Dip and Lion Rock you will come across a small area devoid of trees. Since there is no sapling regrowth it is unlikely that this clearing was formed by logging operations. It is probably a result of the very wet ground, inhibiting tree growth. The plants with the large leaves are called cunjevoi (*Alocasia macrorrhiza*). They thrive on the extra light and moisture found here. The young side stems of the plant were an important food for the Aborigines. In its raw form the plant is highly poisonous, but the Aborigines would repeatedly pound and bake the plant until it had lost its toxicity.

On the far left-hand side of the clearing (the track skirts to the right) stands a small specimen of the giant stinging tree, *Dendrocnide excelsa*. Don't touch! The leaves are covered with fine hairs which can cause extreme pain if touched. Irritation from the sting may last for many weeks. The family name for this plant sounds quite appropriate—*Urticaceae*.

As you emerge from the next track try to find Lion Rock, so-named as the rock is shaped like the head of a lioness. To help you find it, look straight across from where you emerge onto the river.

The next feature to look out for is the Pool of Reflections. According to some of the local old timers, the best time to see the magnificent Pool of Reflections is in the morning light. Sometimes the pools are filled with gravel by violent floods and then perhaps the next flood will clear them again.

Along the track from the Pool of Reflections you will see a grove of sassafras (*Doryphora sassafras*) saplings. Timber getters cleared this area and the sassafras has been quick to take over. The stronger saplings will survive, while the weaker ones will die. Also along the track you will see old stumps of trees up to three metres tall. The notches in the stumps were used to hold the timber getters' planks. The axemen would then stand on the planks to enable them to cut the tree above the buttresses.

Further along the track is a huge example of a strangling fig. Many species of rainforest figs display this strangling characteristic. The seed of the fig latches onto the tree after being deposited by a bird. Roots grow down to the ground and it then starts to grow around the host tree, strangling it in the process. Eventually the tree dies and by the time it rots away the fig is able to support itself. The fig in this case has emerged from the forest canopy.

Rocky Crossing's rock is composed of mudstone. A flood in 1987 gouged out a large amount of rock from the waterfall. The water used to fall almost straight from the pool behind into the pool below.

On the return trip see if you can spot some 'red gold'—the red cedars that have survived the timber getter's axe. They have a grey or brown scaly bark and are one of the few deciduous native trees.

Chichester State Forest Walks

Chichester State Forest is a large area on Barrington's southern slopes. It encompasses the Telegherry River basin (map 2), a source of the Karuah River to the east, together with other forests further west (see Gilwinga Track, map 3). Like most state forests it has numerous old forest roads; most accessible to all types of vehicles, some closed but available for walking. This makes the forest a popular picnic and camp site for Hunter Valley residents.

Walking tracks are not a forestry specialty; they are mainly an adjunct to the picnic areas. So all but Gilwinga are short walks of less than 2 kilometres. Quite frankly picnickers underuse existing tracks, and walking enthusiasts tend to visit national parks. It need not be so, for forestry areas contain some excellent walking environments.

The following walking tracks and heritage features are within Telegherry River section of Chichester State Forest (Map 2). Some locations are close to known Aboriginal sites and artefacts finds.

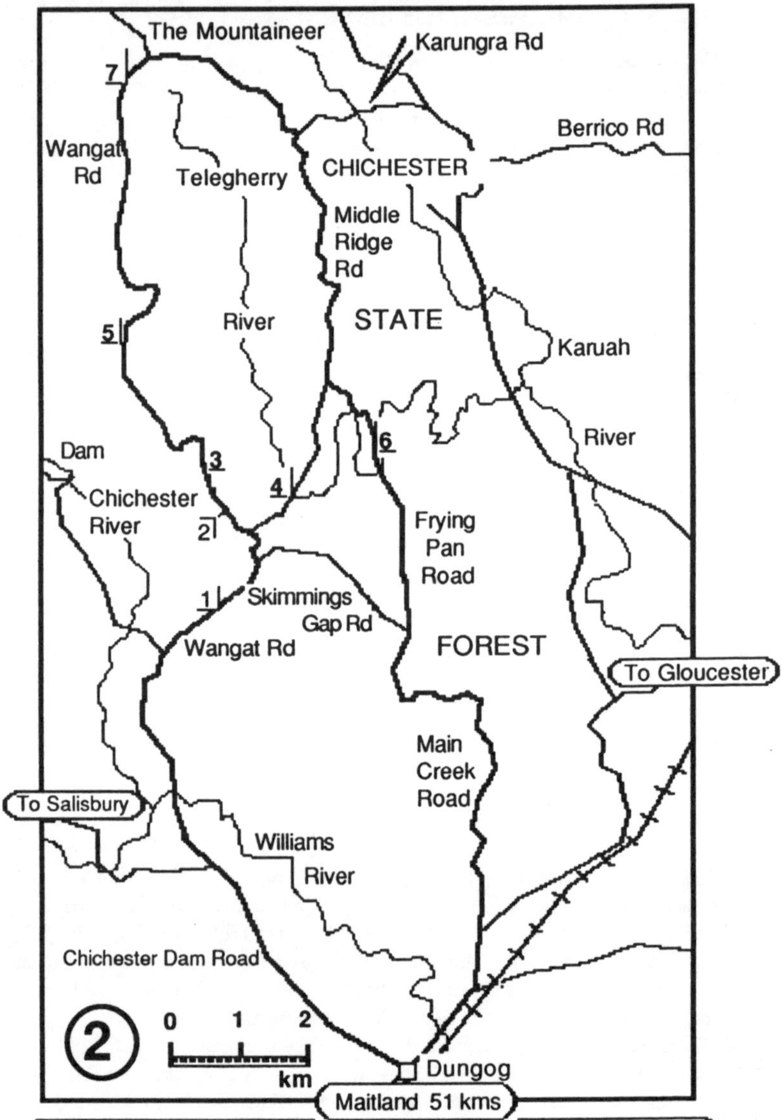

Chichester State Forest Walks

1. Jerusalem Creek Walking Trail is a two-kilometre walking track through various eucalypt forest and subtropical rainforests. Look out for the coachwoods, a species otherwise missing from the southern rainforests. An enchanting walk over a short distance the trail has labelled points of interest. A small parking area at the start of the trail appears only a few kilometres after turning off the Chichester Dam Road. Further information may be found at the parking area, where leaflets are left in a dispenser.

2. Jerusalem Creek Forest Park is actually a picnic area with tables, fireplaces and toilets. It also provides a second access to the Jerusalem Creek walking track. Other walking tracks and a scenic waterfall should be visited too.

3. A Logging Museum. Anyone who's read Les Murray's poem 'In a working forest…' might find themselves moved to take a lingering look at old logging machinery. Here you'll find a petrol driven log hauler, a dobbie and a section of a bullock drawn log jinker.

4. Telegherry Forest Walk. A popular picnic and camping area. It also includes pleasant walking tracks into the forest and along a creek off the Telegherry River. It has some grand forest flora.

5. Dundungra Falls Walk and Chichester Arboretum. A walking track has been laid out through the Arboretum and various tree species have been labelled. A signpost 100 metres before you enter indicates another short track to the foot of Dundungra Falls on Hotel Creek.

6. Frying Pan Creek Forest Walk. Principally a picnic and camping area, it includes a pleasant circular walking track along a minor creek off the Telegherry River.

7. Antarctic Beech Forest. This the southernmost extent of the antarctic beech (*Nothofagus moorei*). This species occurs in cool, moist sites as far north as the McPherson Range in Queensland. Other species occur in temperate rainforest in Tasmania, New Zealand and southern South America, a distribution suggesting a connection with the megacontinent of Gondwanaland. Directly accessible by car, the forest is an opportunity to experience the habitat of this species.

Burraga and Cabre Bald Walks

Apart from rainforests, the Barrington Tops region has eucalyptus forests on the high ridges and slopes. Two other regional peculiarities are Mt Cabre Bald grassland and Burraga Swamp. At present Cabre Bald has no track access.

Cabre Bald is a high 12 ha. area of grassland inhabited by a spectacular community of grass trees, *Xanthorrhoea australis*. It contains some of tallest known of this species in NSW, some up to 2000 years old. Access is via the Basin Road and Mt Allyn road.

Burraga Swamp (Map 3) is a high swamp set amongst antarctic beech. The swamp has a fluctuating water level but no outlet stream. A number of intriguing theories have been put forward for the swamp's formation, but it appears likely that it was the result of a landslide from nearby Mount Leumeah. An excellent track winds from near Mt Allyn through beech and other forest to the swamp. There are interpretive signs placed along the track.

The Gillwinga Track

This track (Map 3) is reached on the Mt Allyn forest road, the same used to reach Burraga Swamp. It is 12 km in length, set amongst spectacular mountain and river environs. Although it is 'closed' it is nevertheless accessible track. Four to six hours of walking time is needed, so allow most of a day to complete the walk.

For the first kilometre stunted eucalypts, mainly messmates (*Eucalyptus obliqua*) are passed. We are starting high, so where the track ventures off the ridge top we quickly meet the antarctic beech rainforests. Afterwards look out for a magnificent view of the Paterson River Valley.

At 1.8 km, a signposted track leads to Mt Leumeah. This is steep and, at times, difficult, but there are views of Burraga Swamp, the Paterson River and Barrington Tops escarpment.

The main track passes the eastern side of Mt Leumeah and onto a saddle before Mt Gunama. Here the cool temperate rainforest gives way to moist eucalypt forest dominated by stately Sydney blue gums and silvertop stringybark. The track then climbs further toward the mountaintop, Mt Gunama (1220 m ASL).

Facing the inevitable descent the track moves to the Allyn River valley, reaching the river at the 5.1 km mark. Here an alternate exit track returns you to Leumeah forest road, where a circular route will return to your car.

If you go further some little gems await, including a charming lunch spot and a swimming hole with large, crystal clear pools. This is the only time the river is crossed. Fern filled gullies, a waterfall and small feeder creeks lie ahead, the track finishes at the Allyn River bridge.

Careys Peak via The Corker

For those who would venture to the Tops the traditional southern access track to Careys Peak climbs The Corker, a mountain standing steeply above Barrington House. Cars are left behind at Lagoon Pinch (see top of Map 1), although the truly athletic might like to start from the Rocky Crossing Track.

Starting from Lagoon Pinch the track is a closed 4wd road. It was only built

3 Gillwinga Track and Burraga Swamp

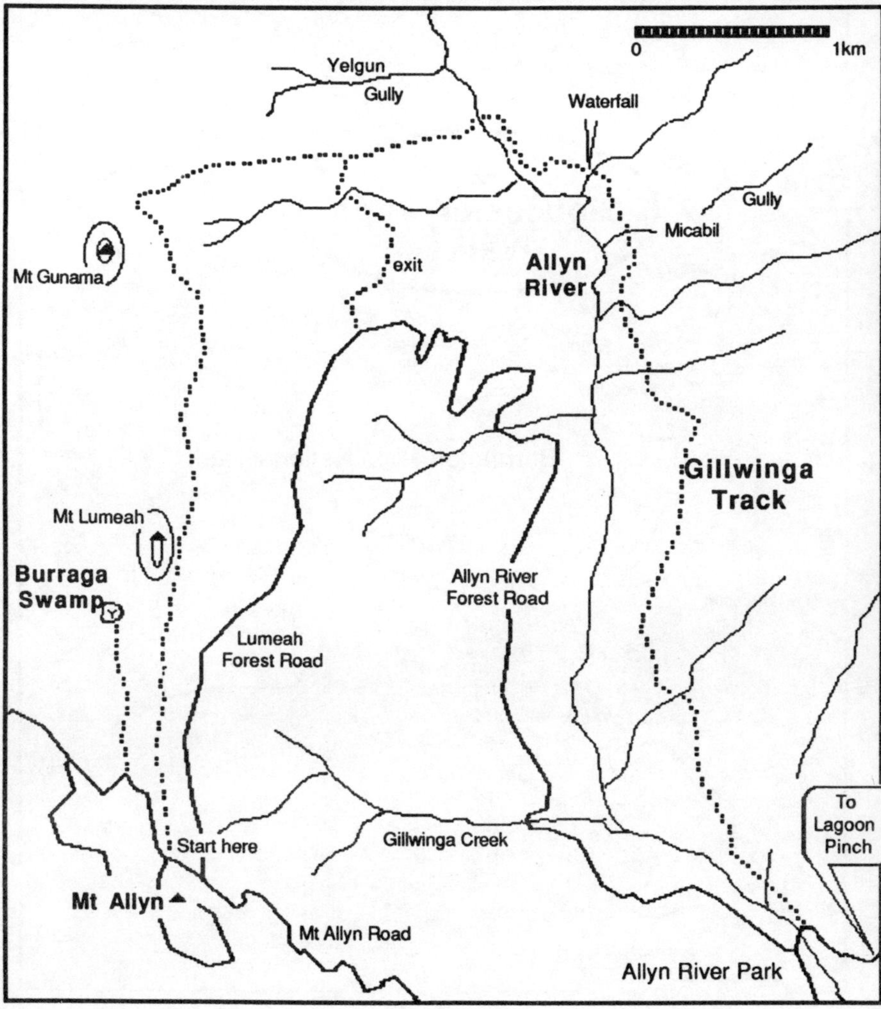

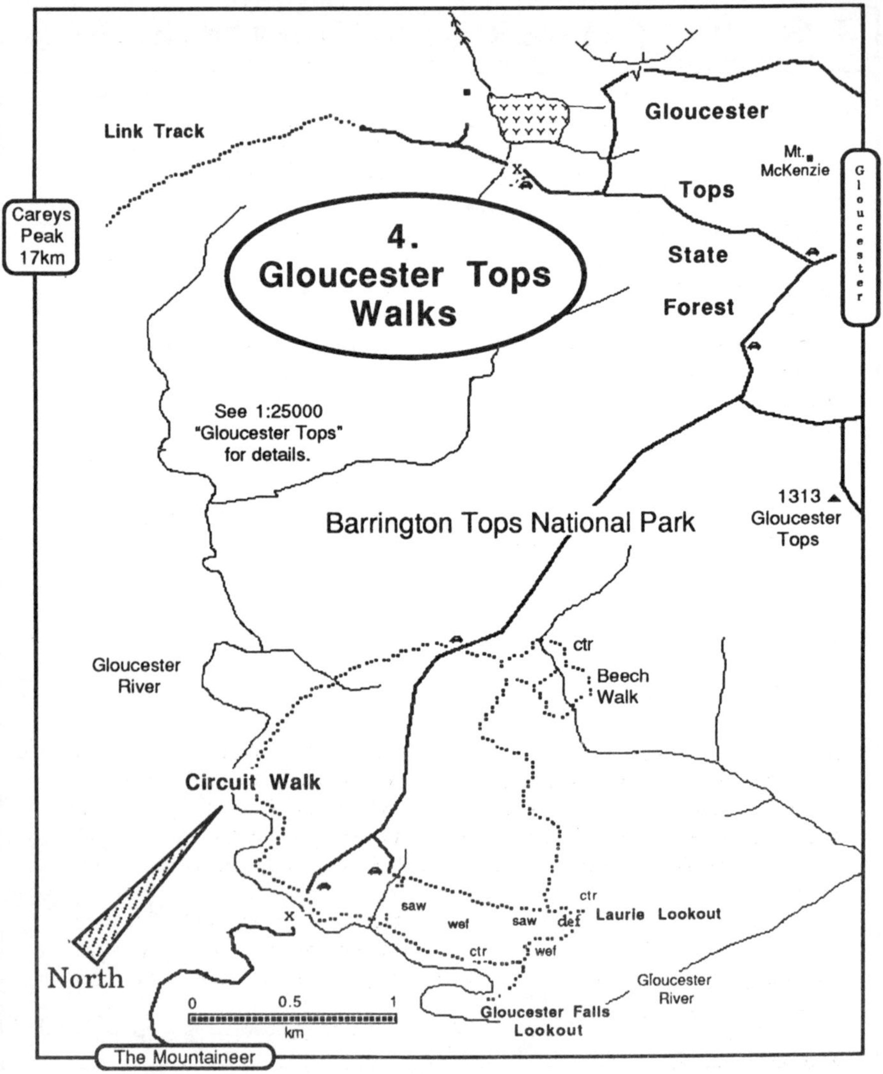
4.
Gloucester Tops
Walks
Link Track
Careys
Peak
17km
Gloucester
Tops
State
Forest
Mt.
McKenzie
Gloucester
See 1:25000
"Gloucester Tops"
for details.
Barrington Tops National Park
1313
Gloucester
Tops
Gloucester
River
ctr
Beech
Walk
Circuit Walk
saw
wef
saw
def
ctr
Laurie Lookout
ctr
wef
North
0
0.5
1
km
Gloucester
River
Gloucester Falls
Lookout
The Mountaineer

in 1957 as a result of local pressures. Its subsequent use caused serious erosion and safety problems as the road is relentlessly steep. With NPWS management it was eventually closed to all vehicles.

In 1970 it snowed on the Tops over the Easter long weekend. I know, as I was walking up the Corker. The snow was quite light, adding a delicacy to the surrounding eucalypt and beech forest. However, I well remember the muddy brown of the track, courtesy of numerous 4wd vehicles. It was sticky sludge with wide pools of thin muddy water, and difficult to negotiate.

We camped inside the now ruined Carey's Peak Hut. Even then the hut was bare floored, with a curious lean to it. But with the exposure of Carey's Peak it was still a useful protection from the extreme cold.

A word of warning: climbing to Careys Peak from the Corker is not for the novice. An 800-metre climb over five kilometres, it is steep and arduous. Little chance of getting lost here, but see Barrington Tops, Map 6, for details of the upper reaches. Every bend brings false hope of relief.

For the masochist walker start from Barrington House on the Rocky Crossing Track. It's a 1250-metre climb to Careys Peak. Climbing the Corker Track to Carey's Peak six times is enough for me. Each time I said to myself 'never again'. I did not climb it a seventh—I discovered the Link Track on Gloucester Tops.

Gloucester Tops

Discovering Gloucester Tops was something of a revelation. To reach Barrington Tops I was told to head towards Gloucester and turn westward 10 km before reaching the township. After 30 km we reached Gloucester River Camping Area. From here a steep forest road climbs (300 to 1150 m ASL) to Gloucester Tops. From the turnoff on the Gloucester-Stroud road (Bucketts Way) the road is mostly unsealed.

The Gloucester Tops comprises the south-eastern arm of the Mt Royal Range. It begins with the sustained climb, past primeval and canopy rainforest, by high and narrow lookouts, skirting the occasional pademelon, snake or wallaby crossing the road.

The Link Track is a gem—there are no persistently steep slopes to negotiate. The moderate climate leaves time and energy to enjoy the surroundings. And aren't they terrific!

Tracks in the area include:

1. the Gloucester Falls track, a 2 km round trip.
2. Gloucester Falls via Beech Track and circle, one way, 3-4 km.
3. Beech Track, full circle, approximately 8 km.

4. a series of off-track walks, from a moderate overland walk on the upper Gloucester River, to a challenging wilderness walk from Gloucester River campsite up to Gloucester Fall (2 full days).

Each of these walks are described below.

Gloucester Falls Walk

Gloucester Top's oldest walking track goes to the scenic heart of the plateau, the Gloucester Falls (see also the NPWS leaflet on Gloucester Tops). Upstream the river has gathered water from numerous swamps, soaks and springs of the subalpine woodlands, grasslands and cool temperate rainforest. At this formative point the river cascades downwards some hundreds of metres into a deep narrow hillside, as remote as can be imagined. 'Falls' is almost a misnomer, as the river winds in a huge 'S' bend, over each metre falling another metre or two. It is impossible to take in a lookout, so the track circles the area, taking in different elements at different points.

The track begins near the picnic and parking area at the end of the Gloucester Tops road (Map 4). Walking in a clockwise direction, you'll pass through a number of different vegetation areas. It is a short, circular walk, and at times it passes near cliff edges, so take care.

From the trackhead to Laurie Lookout you walk through subalpine woodland (shown in the map as SAW). The plants here are adapted to grow in high, cold and exposed areas; snow gums or white sally (*Eucalyptus pauciflora*), mountain gums (*E. dalrympleana*), snow grass and lomandra with its blade-like leaves.

As you walk you may notice patterns in the bush; for instance, the scribble patterns on the trunks of the snow gums. The scribbles are made by insects which live and feed under the bark. Look for the contrast between young eucalypt seedlings and mature trees.

Often the seedlings, such as those of mountain gum, have round leaves growing opposite each other on the stem, while the trees have the familiar narrow leaves arranged alternately on the stem.

There are marked changes in the soil colour in the area, too. These changes are particularly clear when the earth is damp. These soils derive from different rock types, the dark soil from basalt, the light soil from granodiorite. The granodiorite is harder than basalt and does not weather so quickly, so boulders appear where the soil changes from basalt to granodiorite derived.

As you near the lookout, you pass from the subalpine woodland to a dry eucalypt forest (shown as 'def' in the map).

The two vegetation zones overlap and for about 100 metres you can see a steady increase in the number of shrubs with hard, dry leaves and the snow gums are replaced by brown barrels (*E. fastigata*) and messmates (*E. obliqua*).

The Laurie Lookout

From this lookout you can see the number of vegetation zones and the rapid change from one to the other which is characteristic of this park. To the north is the antarctic beech (*Nothofagus moorei*) forest (shown as 'trf'), a type found in cool and temperate, rainy climates. The forest grows on this slope because the aspect protects it from drying winds and sunlight.

The big hill on the far side of the valley shows three forest types. At the bottom of the slope, where most of the run-off accumulates, are warm temperate rainforest species, showing as dark and varied greens. In the middle is wet eucalypt forest ('wef') and at the top, where the slope retains little water and is more exposed, is the dry eucalypt forest ('def').

You can investigate more closely the difference between wet and dry eucalypt forest where the track runs along a boundary between these two forest types.

But soon the wet forest dominates and continues to the Falls Lookout. The brown barrel and messmate grow taller here than in the dry forests and you may see the soft, spreading leaf crown of young beeches.

The Falls Lookout

The land here is very steep, so take care, particularly with children.

As you come onto the lookout area the vegetation changes again. In this exposed area and shallow soil, plants are adapted to dry, infertile conditions. But there is a great variety of plant life here.

The banksias growing below the lookout are unusually large for this species. They can be distinguished from other trees in the area by the large, woody fruits. The woody cases protect the seeds during fires. Then heat from the fire may cause the case to open and the seed falls onto the ash-covered ground, a good place to germinate. From this lookout you have a fine view of one of the many waterfalls of the Gloucester River.

Along the river you again walk through beech forest ('trf'). Many mosses and lichens grow here on the damp rocks and logs. You may see about twenty varieties in a small area.

The river has good swimming spots for summer—and winter, if you like swimming in melted snow. The beech forest ends in a shallow gully. As you move out of the shady, protected areas preferred by the beech, the subalpine woodlands predominate.

The walk continues through a variety of vegetation types. Keep exploring and looking around, there is always something to see in this diverse area.

The Beech Forest Walk

Two kilometres to the north is the intimate Beech Forest Track. For sheer delight and enchantment this short walk into antarctic beech forest and mountain stream can't be beaten. Explore, taste the water, cross the stream. Go as far as you wish. The trails loop back to other sections. From here you can use a new track to link with Laurie Lookout and the Gloucester Falls walk. If you like you can do the entire Gloucester Tops loop walk.

The Gloucester Tops Circuit Walk

For a longer walk taking in both the previous walks there is now a circuit walk. This the best walk of all. You see both of the shorter walks and get the pleasure of exercising the body and relaxing the mind all rolled into one experience.

The walk is only a recent addition. Linking the Beech Walk to the falls is particularly interesting as it passes through variable terrain and transitional vegetation forms. Amongst the most impressive is a forest of old banksias—some 20 metres tall, an extraordinary height for a shrub. There are only moderate slopes to negotiate.

Upstream from the falls a track continues to follow the river into open, treeless terrain, with occasional subalpine woodland, mainly snow gums. After skirting the river environs the route returns to the road immediately opposite the Beech Forest Walk's parking area.

The Link Track

For a long day or overnight walk, this track provides a delightful exploration of high beech forests and subalpine woodlands (SAW), topped off by a magnificent view from Careys Peak. It is one way and 21 km in length, but unlike the Corker, it is only moderately sloped. A NPWS leaflet is available for this track. Allow six hours, or one day. An overnight stay at Wombat Creek is recommended.

It is advisable to take 1:25 000 maps—Barrington and Gloucester Tops, as the map supplied here does not show topography.

The five hour trek starts from a newly erected locked gate. Walking 500 metre along forest road brings you to the 'old' parking area set amongst tall messmates and mountain gums. This is dry eucalypt forest which soon merges into a beech forest (cool temperate rainforest). These two forest types alternate, with the young beech saplings varying in appearance depending on how sheltered their upbringing has been. Some look old and gnarled, whilst others are straight and fresh.

The track rises and drops over small hills or bumps that are made of granodiorite—a granular rock with visible mineral crystals. The harder granodiorite protrudes from the faster weathering basaltic soils.

Beech forest is dominant for the next hour or more, followed by dry, and remarkably open, eucalypt forest and subalpine woodland. Have a look for club moss in this area. It was the second plant group to evolve; an ancestor of all gymnosperms (conifers, etc.).

The variations in vegetation here are caused by the climate. In some places the cold has produced a typical floor area of snow grass and *Lomandra* species, yet in sheltered areas there is a dry eucalypt understorey. A lot of mosses and lichens grow on the rocks along this route.

Listen carefully and you will hear a waterfall that is well worth a visit. About half an hour past the waterfall, the beech trees become more and more stunted until eventually the forest ends altogether.

Because the area further on is quite protected, some beech and other rainforest plants invade the dense undergrowth of the woodland.

The track divides but will later rejoin. The left route is more interesting and more gradually inclined. It passes above a small swamp on the left, and sphagnum moss set amongst a little forest on the right. Again the antarctic beech dominates, with walls of tree ferns appearing overhead, growing in abundance above track cuttings.

All of the Link Trail was once 4wd track. This is evident when a small dam is met beside the track, a remnant water supply for forestry vehicles and the like. Since the track's closure (probably in 1969) its origins have been obscured.

After passing downhill, the track eventually swings up again. Note the mountain stream only 20 metres below the track. Well worth a visit for water and a rest. Subalpine woodland increases once a locked gate is passed. Snow gums dominate the fairly sparse tree cover, with a shrublike native fig species offering edible fruits in summer months.

The walk has taken us to higher ground now, and soon takes a rare dip towards Wombat Creek. You may notice minor fishermen's track on your right as you pass downhill. This heads towards the Barrington River. In the vicinity it is common to find pig traps set up by the NPWS.

The Gloucester River Camping Area

Gloucester River camping area is below Gloucester Tops. A NPWS leaflet is available for this area. It is beside the Gloucester River, approximately 31 km from the turnoff on the Gloucester-Stroud road. The road is largely unsealed, and the last 15 kilometres include nine (normally safe) river crossings.

The camping area (Map 5) was originally a cattle camp, one of about 70 used by a local landowner. Materials for a house and shed were brought to the isolated spot by the bullock teams used by timber getters. The owner established a base, with cooking and other household items, emergency food supplies and an orchard of a hundred odd orange, mulberry, loquat, peach and plum trees.

When a road was built, the last kilometre through impressive and dense rainforest, it became popular with campers. The landowner welcomed the campers but unfortunately was repaid for his courtesy by repeated acts of theft and vandalism. The area is still a campsite, now part of discrete section of the park. The house, shed, and most of the fruit trees have been removed and the area is slowly returning to its natural state. The remaining stockyards and the old bullock dray are rustic reminders of earlier days.

Gloucester River Waterlife. As mentioned earlier, rivers create openings in the forest, allowing a passage for air, water and sunlight. When the water is moving fast, such as here, it rapidly absorbs oxygen from the air. But oxygen content is often quite low in still ponds, so the animals living here must have adaptations to cope. Some gulp air on the water's surface. Some carry bubbles of air around with them, like the water boatman, which has special hairs to trap air bubbles. Others have many branched gills. The exceptional blood worm absorbs oxygen from the water directly into its blood pigment.

With both a pond and a river nearby the area is an ideal spot for discovering the animals living in waters of high and low oxygen content[11]. On hot days, for example, you may see many more animals close to the water surface, especially in the pond. This is because hot water holds less oxygen than cold and the animals come to the surface for air.

Some of these pond animals are carnivorous, and hunt organisms in the water or catch insects which fall to surface of the pond. The back swimmer (it really does swim on its back), the water boatman and water strider are all carnivorous. You may see water striders on the surface in busy groups which scatter in all directions if disturbed.

To look closer at the animals, you can scoop them up with a fine net or a cup, or gently lift up a stick or log. But please remember to keep water creatures in the water and always put things back as you found them.

Some river animals have adaptations which enable them to live in fast flowing water. They have suckers, hooks or claws to cling to rocks or vegetation. Some have a streamlined shape and small, plate-like gills which are resistant to damage. The dragonfly nymph controls its direction of movement in flowing water by forcing water from its rectum, like a jet.

Many of these river dwellers hide under rocks, and you may see them if you gently turn over the rocks. You might see a collection of stones stuck together. The architect of this home is the caddis fly larva. In still water it makes a lighter home of sticks.

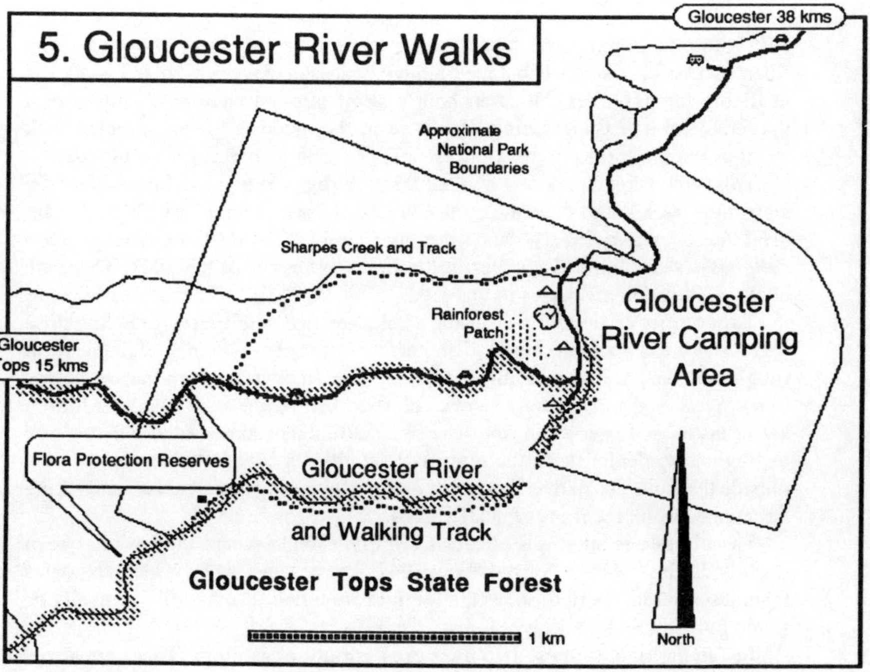
5. Gloucester River Walks
Gloucester 38 kms
Approximate National Park Boundaries
Sharpes Creek and Track
Rainforest Patch
Gloucester River Camping Area
Gloucester Tops 15 kms
Flora Protection Reserves
Gloucester River and Walking Track
Gloucester Tops State Forest
1 km
North

Although the animals appear spiny in drawings, most of them are quite soft, as the water supports them without the need for a strong skeleton. So please handle with care, and once again, remember to leave things as you found them.

Sharpes Creek Walk

Just before you reach the Gloucester River camping area there is a walk along Sharpes Creek, a small tributary of the Gloucester River (a NPWS leaflet is available for this track). It is an hour's stroll through charming landscape; a moderate but satisfying outing. If you're in the mood, a longer, circular walk requires more effort to reach Gloucester Tops forest road. Return via the road.

This walk takes you along a creek through regenerating rainforest. Near the sign at the track's start there are quite a few paperbarks, mostly prickly paperbark (*Melaleuca stypheliodes*), and the pink-tipped bottlebrush (*Callistemon salignus*). Many ferns also occur in the first few metres of the walk. There are about eight different species in this area.

Twenty metres up, almost on the track, are two small trees growing close together. One is about 20 cm in diameter; the other about 5 cm in diameter with rough bark and a line winding around it. The smaller tree is a native cherry (*Exocarpus* spp.), so-called because the stem behind the seed swells to form a sweet-tasting red fruit when ripe. The first settlers sent some of these fruits back to England to demonstrate the primitive nature of a country where seeds grew outside the fruit. The native cherry is a root parasite, attaching itself to, and taking sustenance from, the roots of nearby trees.

The big tree is an acacia. Acacias are often found where the land has been disturbed. This area was logged about 1947. The acacia's size shows that it dates from just after this period, so, as the rainforest returns, acacias will eventually be found only in the dry eucalypt forest.

Just to the right of these two trees grow groups of saplings. These are also a sign of past tree-felling, as they would not be so dense if a mature rainforest canopy was overhead.

In some places you will notice animal paths. These animals use the track when humans are not around. You will probably see some scratchings. Lyrebirds scratch up the leaves and bandicoots make conical holes about 10 cm wide. The scratchings of native mice (*Antechinus* spp.) are similar to bandicoots, but smaller.

About 13 metres downstream from the first creek crossing is a kangaroo apple (*Solanum* sp.), a shrub which has violet blue flowers and orange-red fleshy fruits.

At the edge of the creek, on the far side, look up into the tree—there you will see epiphytes and mosses growing on a branch. The huge smooth barked tree on the right as you come out of the creek is a blue gum (*E. salignus*). From here on you are walking along the boundary between the rainforest beside the creek and the eucalypt forest of the drier hillside.

Mosses are common here. Bend down and get an ant's eye view of these forests of tiny plants, representatives of some of the oldest plant groups on earth.

Birdlife thrives here. The grey fantail is a curious bird and common in this area. It will often come to look you over, landing a few feet away. If convinced that you mean no harm, if you are quiet and move slowly, it will continue to feed as if you were not present. The bird is an aerial acrobat, catching insects on the wing amongst the shrub branches. It is a small grey bird with a tail which opens out into a fan when manoeuvring. You may also find a diamond python snake, sunning itself after a good meal, possibly a fantail!.

Near the end of the walk, look for a grass tree (*Xanthorrhoea* sp.) The sap from these plants was once used as a varnish, so many were exported to Europe. In some areas on the eastern coast the plants were wiped out and have not re-established.

At the sign, you can go up the steep section to the road. If you do not mind the grade, it is will worth the walk to compare dry eucalypt forest with rainforest.

Watch out for vehicle traffic if returning via the road. Try looking down on the forest; you may be able to identify some of the trees you've recently passed.

Gloucester Upriver Walk and Trek (allow at least 2 days)

When I recall a walk up the Gloucester River gorge it is with some awe and affection. The first section along old forestry track is pleasant indeed; beyond it is as wild and as rugged as anywhere I've been.

Your walk begins from the camp site. The river is first crossed upstream. From here it is straightforward (but never dull) walking for several kilometres before another crossing. Soon after a clearing shows an old forest cabin, long in decline. The route progressively becomes closed by jungle.

To continue it becomes necessary to walk in the river, a course of action two of us took some years ago. We continued all the way to Gloucester Falls. This involved some truly challenging elements. In places climbing equipment would have been appropriate.

The narrow gorge, mountain streams and untouched rainforests are most satisfying.

A word of warning though: this trek takes a full two days to complete, and could take more. The final ascent is also a little daunting.

Strolls around Camp

The Gloucester River itself is a key attraction for visitors: its sounds, the surrounds, the swimming, perhaps liloing too—all these are inviting. Perhaps you'll try a walk up or down stream, or explore a track on the opposite bank. Just lying around on the bank, soaking up sun, will probably afford the sight of an animal coming for a drink.

Here though, are two other suggested strolls around camp: the day stroll, and a night stroll.

A Little Day Stroll. The day stroll is an attempt to overcome a inner taboo. As you camp in one of the official campsites you're bound to be close to the rainforest. Why is it so rarely visited? (I have never seen anyone visiting it). It is like a dark, locked room. You live in the house, but no one enters. Let's break the taboo, and enter.

What's in there? It is dark and quiet. Perhaps you've heard the occasional animal sounds scattering leaf litter. Peer in. Look at the ground; it is remarkably rocky. You may need to give your eyes time to adjust. Look for the ground vegetation; there is practically none. OK, let's go in. You'll need to step carefully over the rocky ground, avoid tangled vines, but otherwise it is easy to progress. In a sense there is little to see; probably less to hear. It is another world, reminding me at least that rainforest grows on poor soils, not rich. It has achieve this habitat over a long period of time, in very specific circumstances. Lots of water, adequate soils, and sun-driven plant life better able than any other to reach out for light.

The junction of Sharpes Creek and the river was also an Aboriginal camp site. Artefact scatters, small rock flakes and other indicators have been archaeologically confirmed. For a Sherlock Holmes fantasy the site is worth exploration. It is imperative that no item found should be disturbed or removed.

A Little Night Stroll. At night, quite a few animals may be seen. A bit of quiet and patience, and a torch, is needed. Then you might see wallabies, pademelons, possums, gliders, bandicoots or marsupial mice. With more patience and stealth you may see rare animals such as the quoll, feathertail glider, lyrebird, parma wallaby, rufous rat kangaroo and New Holland mouse.

There is no need to go far; just a stroll around the camp tracks and environs will be sufficient.

Barrington Tops

Walking over a subalpine plateau of the Tops is easy; it's an undulating

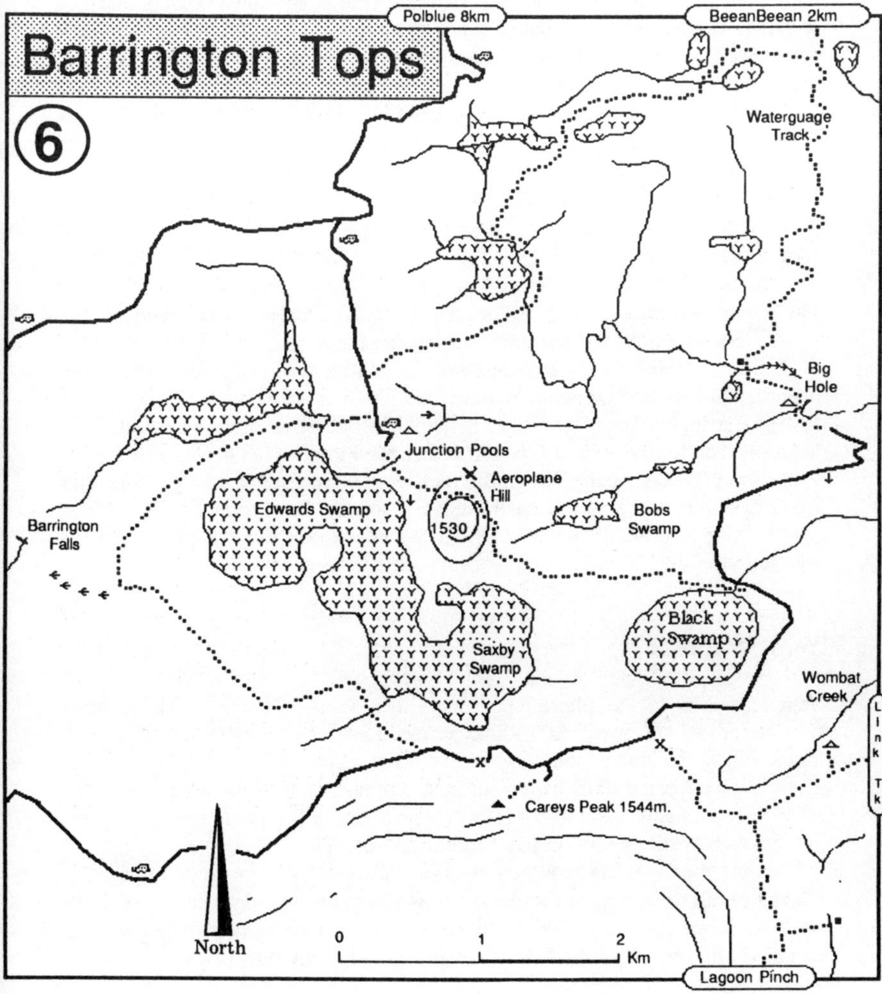
Barrington Tops
6
Polblue 8km
BeeanBeean 2km
Waterguage Track
Big Hole
Junction Pools
Aeroplane Hill
Edwards Swamp
1530
Bobs Swamp
Barrington Falls
Black Swamp
Saxby Swamp
Wombat Creek
Link Tk
Careys Peak 1544m.
North
0
1
2
Km
Lagoon Pinch

countryside of frost hollows, creeks, swamps, peat bogs and woodland, ideal for walking. Covering 30 km daily is possible, though I prefer to walk smaller distances. Linger to take in the features of the area. Allow yourself the pleasures of curious and patient observation.

On-track or off-track walking is possible, though off-track walking is frustrated by the effects of the scotch broom infestation. On-track walking is considerable, though much of it is the track is 4wd.

Access by Foot

The Barrington Plateau is accessible to walkers from three main directions:

1. From the north, Polblue via Beean Beean Plain.

2. From the south, Lagoon Pinch near the Williams River, some 43 km from Dungog. Access to Barrington House is well known but access to the Tops less so. See Barrington Tops National Park map. Most of the access road is sealed. As mentioned earlier vehicles can be left at Lagoon Pinch.

3. From the east, using The Link Track from Gloucester Tops via Gloucester River camping area, some 31 km west of Gloucester. The Gloucester Tops forest road is open to normal vehicles, but should be avoided during, and soon after, wet periods.

Vehicle Access

Vehicle access to the plateau is from either Scone, 70 km away, or from Gloucester, 50 km away. At Polblue access outward is suitable only for 4wd, taking either the Barrington and Polblue trails, either side of Polblue Swamp. These trails are particularly dangerous in, and immediately after, wet weather. The NPWS recommends that visitors refrain from entering at these times. Entry gates are locked between 1 June and 30 September inclusive.

The weather here can be severe. Sections of 'black soil' roads are impassable when wet. Lives have been lost through misadventure and unpreparedness. Even 4wds have become bogged in the 'black soil' or treacherous clay mudpools. In fact anything less than a 4wd is not recommended at any time of year.

European Incursions

Yet despite the difficulty of access and forbidding climate there is a history of European habitation long before the coming of jeeps and 4wd.

Foresters, goldminers, hunters fishermen and ranchers have all occupied the

Tops—admittedly some, like the gold diggers, only nibbled at the edges. At Copeland, for example, some 3000 people mined the lower valley in the 1870s. Foresters after beech, eucalypt and other timbers cut down trees on the Tops, but found the slopes more lucrative. Even hunters who came to the Tops may perhaps have done better in the earlier years on the slopes or in the valleys, as wildlife, too, found the severe high climate forbidding.

Water is the lifeblood of the Tops. So it was the cattle ranchers who seasonally visited the Tops before the creation of the national park. Perhaps it was due partially to cheap leases, or perhaps only seasonal droughts on the lower slopes drove landowners to higher ground. But come they did, and this produced the first 'tracks' into the Tops.

Today, visitors are largely walkers, four-wheel-drivers or fishing enthusiasts.

The first and only permanent homestead was built on Edwards Plain, close to Junction Pools. It was disassembled and removed in the 1960s when the park was created.

Introduced Species

On your walk around the Tops you may notice ground disturbance or diggings. This damage is caused by feral pigs turning the soil over to look for worms and plant roots. Consequently park staff are involved in a trapping program to eradicate this animal. Feral horses and foxes are also considered a nuisance.

Scotch Broom

Scotch broom (*Cytisus scoparius*) is a worse infestation, currently growing in about 10,000 ha of private property, state forest and national park. On the plateau, it forms impenetrable thickets in some places, taking over existing vegetation and sheltering feral pigs. It seriously affects grazing, forest regeneration, recreation and conservation value.

At present it is mainly restricted to the Barrington Tops plateau but it is feared that the plant could become more adapted to lower elevations given its vigour and ability to produce large numbers of long lived seeds. There are signs of this happening already, with small infestations in two remote areas of Gloucester Tops and lower sections of the Barrington River.

Broom is a noxious weed in many areas of Australia's eastern states, in New Zealand and California. Unfortunately Barrington Tops is considered to have the most virulent infestation in Australia, with about 30% of the 10,000 ha. infestation on the plateau in the form of dense growth. This percentage is increasing annually (see the NPWS leaflet on the Scotch broom threat).

It is easily recognised: it is deciduous, and has a bright yellow pea flower that covers the plant around November. The stems are green and multi-ribbed with small green leaves growing along their length. Starting as a single shoot, much like lucerne, it progresses from being a multi-stemmed, upright shrub to a large, grey-trunked bush up to five metres high.

The plant's ability to increase and multiply is daunting. It produces numerous pods which contain hard, shiny, dark-green seeds about 4 mm long. The pods are green when growing and dark brown to black when mature. The pods eject seeds up to three metres from the parent plant, with each plant producing up to 6000 seeds per year. They are easily dispersed via streams, mud or vehicles, walkers boots and in the manure of stock and feral animals.

Currently there is no long term control method. Herbicide spraying is being used to contain the plant as much as possible on the plateau until a long term biological control is found. The movement and cleanliness of machinery are also controlled. Control is possible in specific areas or with isolated infestations.

Herbicide will kill the plant effectively. Follow-up spraying before new plants seed is essential (within two to three years). Burning the year following spraying will help germinate seed for subsequent spraying. The plant must be in leaf for spraying to be successful.

During winter, broom can be slashed successfully. It can be dug out (with difficulty) and is sensitive to fire.

However the cost for all these methods is high, so biological control is being investigated. The Barrington Tops Broom Council is encouraging research. An agent was due to be released in the summer of 1991-2. Let's hope for its complete success, so that Bald Hill, near Edwards Swamp, is once again bald.

Aboriginal Habitation

Aboriginal habitation of the Tops has not been researched. Only nearby sites indicate any sign of past habitation. No one appears to know which particular tribe or tribes held territory here.

Barrington's geographical barrier is formidable. Adverse climatic conditions for most of the year probably ensured only seasonal habitation, to harvest fruit in late summer.

Features of the Tops

Before moving to the walks here are a number of features of the Tops. You might wish to use the Tops map to orientate yourself to each place.

Careys Peak. At 1544 metres above sea level Careys Peak is one of the higher points on the Barrington Plateau, and certainly has the most spectacular views.

From the peak you can look down the Allyn River and into the Hunter Valley and even see Newcastle on a clear, windy day.

If you look west you will see the defined edge of the escarpment. Notice the sharp line between the beech forest and the subalpine woodlands on top. Looking north to the park you can see how frost hollows patchwork the area. Often the park is surrounded by clear skies even though a mass of clouds is above the plateau. As the air rises over the plateau it cools, forming clouds.

The Barrington Bogs. Edwards Swamp, Bob's Swamp, Brumlow, Saxbys and Black Swamp; these are the largest bogs found north of the Kosciusko National Park. Unfortunately their naming as 'swamps' conjure visions of muddy, depressing masses of reeds and rotting vegetation. How unjust! The Tops bogs are subalpine peat watercourses—the world's finest filters.

The subalpine bogs have another distinction: they have been accumulating organic debris, or peat, for thousands of years. As such they provide a valuable record of the plants that have inhabited the area.

They are aesthetically pleasing too. With variations of greens, greys, purples and indigos they are expansive features set at a formidable height. The tussock grasslands and woodlands present a wild space only paralleled by sections of the Snowy Mountains.

Crash of the Mosquito Bomber. During WW II a mosquito bomber crashed on 'Aeroplane Hill' at 1500 m ASL. All hands were killed. It is only one of a number of crashes on the Tops. Some have never been found. I believe the bomber's propeller now hangs in Barrington House.

Selby Alley Hut. The hut was built in 1955 by the Newcastle Bushwalking Club. All the building materials were carried in by hand from the Polblue end—the Corker road had not yet been built. Selby Alley's contribution was so generous that the hut was named after him.

The hut is there with the NPWS's blessing. The Service appreciates that it is a useful emergency shelter. Those who wish to use it should ensure that there is no damage to the surroundings. Everyone is welcome to use the hut, however a contribution should be left (or sent directly to the Newcastle Bushwalking Club) so they can meet the costs of upkeep and repairs.

The rainforest, the stream and hut are impressive; but of course the facilities are quite spartan. A journal, or the ubiquitous 'pet rat' (native of course) can be night time entertainment.

Junction Pools. This is perhaps the easiest campsite to reach by 4wd or by foot. The site is excellent. Open and slightly sloping, it is in and downstream from Edwards Swamp. There is a fine swimming hole nearby, it is close to Aeroplane Hill and the crash site, and there are numerous possible on- and off-track walks.

On-track we have the Pools to Beean Beean plain, the loop to Careys Peak via Aeroplane Hill or Edwards Plains. All are described.

Off-track, people may wander down the Barrington River. Broom infestations must be negotiated. However, downstream, where the rapids cease, it is possible to lilo for around two kilometres. As well it is also possible to skirt Edwards Swamp for a direct route to Careys Peak. It is not faster though.

Big Hole. A unfortunate name for an unusual Tops feature. The Barrington River is an idyllic mountain stream on the Tops. It is young, its waters gathered from the surrounding peat swamps, and has a moderate gradient with occasional ponds—which makes it ideal for gentle liloing.

In the later, more remote sections the river plunges steeply downwards. Before this is Big Hole, where the stream comes to sudden halt besides a granite outcrop. A pond collects the river waters, only this pond is round, deep and bordered by soil, not rocks. I am happy to speculate on its stature as a place of significance for Aborigines, despite its remote location.

Apart from a pleasant stroll around the granite outcrop, off track walking downstream is made difficult by dense vegetation.

An Aeroplane Hill walk via Bob's Swamp is an better. For another deviation veer off the 4wd track before Black Swamp to discover antarctic beech and other groves and curiosities.

Beean Beean Plain. The plain is a volcanic plug, uplifted over millions of years. It is high, so there is only shallow soil formation. Its openness to extremes of weather means it supports a large open grassland community. Prior to national park formation was used for summer cattle grazing. Now it is more likely to provide feed for brumbies, kangaroos, wombats, etc.

Barrington Tops Walks

For the following six walks we assume a northern entry to the plateau. They can be linked to make a more or less complete trek of the plateau using the existing track system. A brochure on the Barrington Tops is available from the NPWS.

Beean Beean Plain to Big Hole (90 mins)

Once the old 4wd track joins the Waterguage track a thick scrub layer joins the usual subalpine woodland (SAW). In particular there are a lot of young saplings, possibly the result of past burning and grazing. The occasional cattle or native animal skull may be found. Further on we pass along the high hills past further

SAW, the occasional high swampy bog and seepage streams. Wet, even at this height!

The track proceeds steadily downhill after the Junction Ponds turnoff. As you pass downhill look out for a natural spring. Keep a eye on the track cuttings, as underneath the overhanging grassy tufts are beautifully disguised bird nests. On reaching the Barrington River next to a weather station cross over, then swing left, following the track to Big Hole camping area. The area around the crossing is worthy overland walk.

Big Hole to Careys Peak (1 hr)

The subalpine woodland throughout this area is complemented by two species of wattle. One of these, *Acacia barringtonensis*, was originally discovered here.

On the way up the hill a side excursion into the beech forest environs is recommended. Here you can meet the occasional large, old gum tree, something not normally associated with this forest type. It is evidence of the continuous shift of forest boundaries. The beech and its associated species have crept up hill, surrounding the former eucalyptus/sclerophyll forest. It begs the question: what has changed over the lifetime of these gums?

Later the track passes around Black Swamp's edge. On the other side of the road, sphagnum moss has grown beneath the leaf litter, giving a spongy surface in places.

Junction Pool to Careys Peak (up to 2 hrs)

There are a number of ways of reaching Careys Peak from Junction Pools. I shall describe a circular walk using two routes: first, from the Pools to Careys Peak via Black Swamp and Aeroplane Hill, returning on the roundabout track skirting Edwards Swamp.

From the Pools cross the Barrington stream either directly or, if you want your feet thoroughly dry, try a little downstream. Ascend Aeroplane Hill. After only 200 metres you'll notice a cairn on left side of the track. If you wish to locate the aircraft remains ignore the mysterious numbering and veer left along the contour for around another 220 metres. Where the hill dips into a flattish area, vine and fern tree jewelled, you'll find the few remains. Do not remove any item.

Otherwise complete the ascent, then follow an equal descent. The track flattens out, passing through broom infested landscape. Along this hilltop you could once go direct to Careys Peak, but not now.

The track meets Black Swamp, then joins the Big Hole 4wd road. It is easy walking from there to Careys.

Careys Peak to Junction Pools (Allow 3 hrs)

The return trip rejoins the 4wd trail, then takes the left fork of the main track. Going down hill you will soon see some small stunted patches of beech forest. It is too exposed for the forest to encroach any further on the plateau at this point.

Approximately 1 km west of the turnoff you leave the 4wd trail and take the Edwards Swamp Walking track. It is signposted, but is nevertheless easy to pass by. Look closely at the grasses and herbs that grow along the track and close to the swamp's edges. In summer their small flowers are worth a closer look, preferably with a x10 magnifying glass.

For fauna, walkers perusing the swamp's edge might also come across the crustacean shells. Further on near some large frost hollows—often incorrectly called plains because of their size—you may spot kangaroos feeding here in the early morning or late afternoon.

Notice how some woodland trees look as if they have been repeatedly cut—more or less horizontally—by an axe. This is caused by a grub called longicorn, the larvae of the long-horned beetle, which feeds on the sapwood of the tree. You'll spot this feature on many trees throughout the park.

Old fences and stock yards may also be seen, reminders of past times when the area was grazed by cattle during the summer months.

Pig traps are also found, laid out by the NPWS. These are ingenious devices that allow the animals to enter but not leave the pen. An introduced species, the pig not only disturbs the ecological balance by its invasion of wombat territory but causes far greater damage to grasses and soils by its systematic and unsightly uprooting of the ground.

A small diversion can be taken to Barrington Falls, a rather grandiose title for a small cascade in the Barrington River's most formative heights. There is no track, but it should be approached from above through relatively open woodland. The point of this walk is as much to spot the variable terrain as to experience the falls. For amongst the harsh frost hollows, swamps and grasslands, the small gullies around the creek house a remarkable variety of species. The tree ferns, for example, are associated more with rainforest and the tropics than Barrington's high altitude. So a descent to the stream's denser vegetation is necessary—and rewarding. But please step lightly —and carefully—as the dense vegetation is both delicate and vengeful!

Returning to the track we circle to the east, in from a wooded hillock, to the left the open frost hollow and Barrington stream. When you reach the Barrington River—newly merged with other small streams—a left turn will lead you to the Barrington Trail, a right turn follows the river and straight ahead leads to the road and walking track. However before this junction is a diversionary track leading back up to the hill you'll just came around. This is where Barrington Top's only 'permanent' homestead once stood. Its materials were removed for further use around twenty years ago.

It is then only a short distance rejoin the 4WD track, and hence to Junction Pools and its delightfully situated swimming hole.

Junction Pools to Beean Beean Plain (2 hrs)

This track, the most direct to Beean Beean, begins by following a horse trail down to Bromlow Creek. Following the creek through the frost hollow and over a swamp and you'll reach perhaps one of the prettiest areas on the Tops. In most circumstances you'll get wet feet; unless conditions are particularly adverse this result should be welcomed!

To make the track more visible there are markers leading across and out of the frost hollow. Climbing the hill the track reaches the top to join another old track. Bromlow Creek is 150 m to the left, again with a waterfall and steps downstream. This is a lovely spot for a picnic.

Turn right and you continue the walk past frost hollows into thick scrub. Because this area is protected from the prevailing winds, shrubs dominate the vegetation instead of grass.

To Wombat Creek (30 min) and **Selby Alley Hut** (1 hour)

Between Black Swamp and Careys Peak is a road, blocked by a locked gate. This was once the access road to the Allyn and Williams rivers (via Lagoon Pinch) and Gloucester Tops (via the Link track). Now both are walking tracks.

For closer destinations there is Wombat Creek, a secluded camp site besides beech forest, a well positioned stopover for anyone wishing to walk the Link Track next day. Around two kilometres away is Selby Alley Hut, which provides good protection in foul weather.

The Northern Access: Polblue

As an introduction to the Tops region, the Polblue entrance is recommended, especially if a later pick up at Gloucester Tops or the Williams River can be organised. It's one way to start the walk at a high altitude, allowing yourself time to get 'in stride' before anything more difficult. Fortunately the walker is blessed with undulating highlands and plains with soft grasses underfoot.

Polblue is close to a number of interesting places to the north, set in state forestry areas. This is remote terrain, and the features, though close to parking areas, are as wild and as enchanting as any.

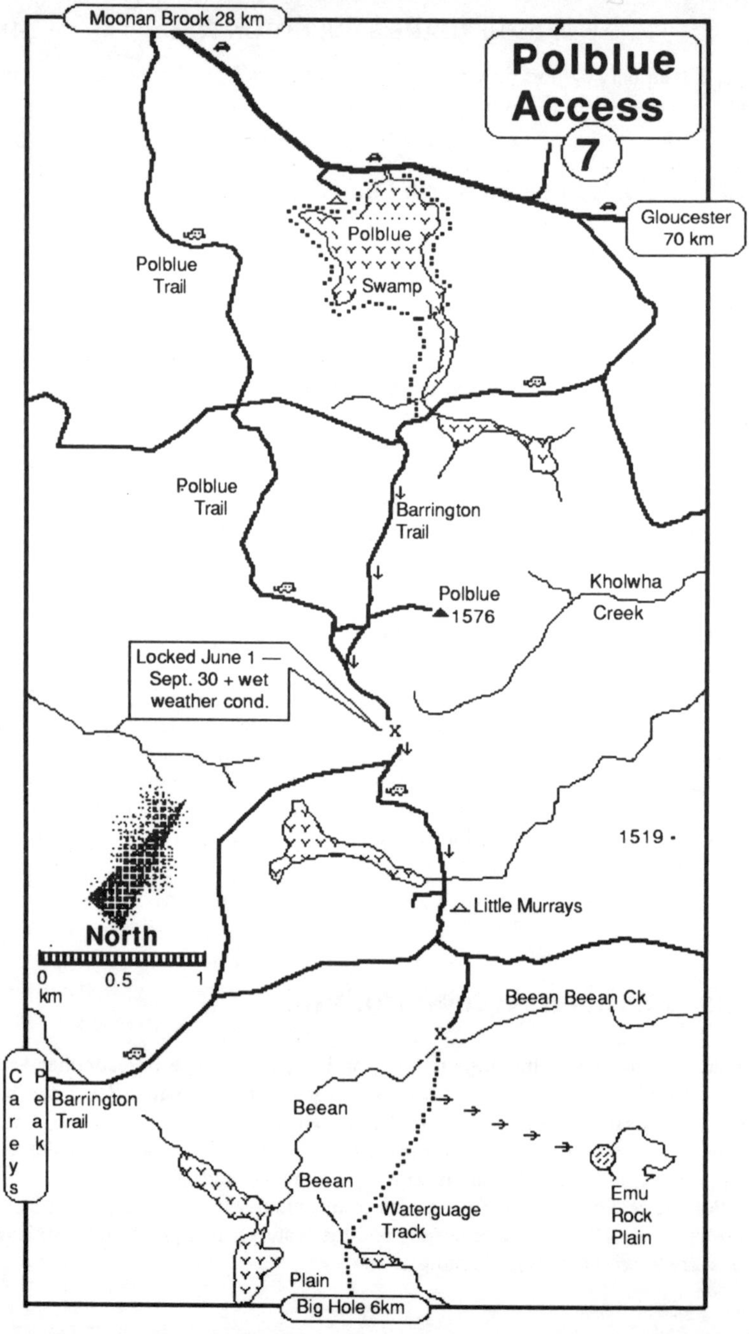

Moonan Brook 28 km
Polblue
Access
7
Gloucester
70 km
Polblue
Swamp
Polblue
Trail
Polblue
Trail
Barrington
Trail
Polblue
1576
Kholwha
Creek
Locked June 1 —
Sept. 30 + wet
weather cond.
1519
Little Murrays
North
0
0.5
1
km
Beean Beean Ck
Careys
Peak
Barrington
Trail
Beean
Beean
Plain
Waterguage
Track
Emu
Rock
Plain
Big Hole 6km

Polblue to Little Murrays (90 mins)

For anyone with a ordinary road vehicle Polblue Swamp is a good starting point for your Barrington Tops sojourn. Simply follow the Forestry track along the Swamp's edge to the southern grassy flat. From here follow upstream on the south western creek bank where it is relatively open. About one kilometre later the 4wd track on the opposite bank will be seen. Cross the stream and join the road to Polblue peak and Little Murrays camp site. The mountain gums start to grow quite thick and tall in this section, creating a rather large subalpine woodland.

A quick visit to Polblue peak is gained by following a vehicular track. Broom infestation is dense here. There is no view either, but you may notice earlier trig point structures and remnant fencing. Continue as shown on the map to Little Murrays, enjoying the grassland, subalpine woodland and tiny beech forest remnants in the gully folds.

To Beean Beean Plain (30 mins)

Little Murrays is a pleasant campsite next to a reliable stream. Wonderful water here. The only facilities are the fireplace and rubbish bin. Direct vehicle access is possible but drivers run extra, and inadvisable, risk if the weather turns foul.

A swing to the left, and then right, then walkers enters the southern edge of Beean Beean Plain. Taste the cool and sweet clear waters of Beean Beean Creek. Beyond is soft snowgrass and Black Sally gum trees with their greenish trunks give the area an parklike appearance. Notice how vehicles have compacted the soil in track's wheel ruts. If you step onto the rut soil and then on the uncompressed soil you will feel the change in sponginess.

Anyone with curiosity and time should take a diversion to Emu Rock. Entering the woodland you'll immediately notice the proliferation of tracks; brumby tracks. They appear to be a collection of numerous well trodden walking tracks.

The broom infestation has created an understorey that once did not exist. However it is still relatively open, with atmosphere strange and eerie. Why? Perhaps it is the stillness of the place, or, more accurately, the collection of sparse sounds, emphasising the whistling winds. Or perhaps it's the dry vegetation, your presence emphasised by the crackling of twigs and dry leaf litter underfoot. Most importantly there is the 'sameness' of the terrain, which is uniformly open forest, largely flat. The walker has no obvious reference point. As you take further steps into it the sense of distance from 'civilisation' can be unnerving. Where am I going? What am I going to see? Why am I doing this to myself? The doubts are well founded, for although it is only a little over a kilometre inland it is remarkable easy to lose your bearings. Take a compass on this one.

Emu Rock is part of Emu Rock Plain. It is a rare dry lagoon where rain waters occasionally flow, forming a shallow water basin built on a rock platform with a clay base. Brumbies commonly congregate here or on the nearby plain. I am yet to see an emu, so perhaps the name refers to an emu-shaped egg or body (with the outlet its neck?).

When retracing your steps, use the brumbies tracks as a guide, as these largely travel between here and Beean Beean.

Major Treks

Longer journeys involving camping require preparation, and it's preferable to go with someone experienced. Planning should give regard to minimising impact on the environment.

Preparation. All walkers should be prepared for sudden changes in weather, particularly on the Tops. Snow storms can arise in a matter of hours, even in summer. A hat is recommended for sunny days, with raingear and other protective clothing a sensible precaution. There is no need to carry much water; it is abundant. However a First Aid Kit, some food, matches and compass could prove invaluable.

For an accurate insight into the region's topography it is advisable to take 1:25,000 maps—Barrington and Gloucester Tops, with Moonan Brook useful for the Polblue section, Chichester and Carrabolla for the southern slopes.

Regulations. The park and forestry regions are intended to be enjoyed without excessive or harmful behaviour. Outdoor experiences are intended for everyone's enjoyment. Considering the damage caused by excessive fires, walkers should use gas cookers wherever possible. Beautifully situated campsites need your careful use. Some sites are provided with bins, but otherwise all rubbish should be carried out. Fires should be lit in official fireplaces, where provided.

Polblue to Gloucester Tops. Combine the Polblue access tracks as entry to the Tops. Combine various walks given, exiting via the Link Trail to Gloucester Tops. This should be about a 70 km trek.

Barrington House to Barrington Tops. A 3-4 day walk, beginning with a monumental climb to the tops. Three or four days is recommended. If a pick-up can be arranged, alternative exits via Polblue to the Link Track are recommended.

Polblue to Dungog via Chichester State Forest and The Mountaineer. Take the Polblue to Gloucester Tops walk, extending it from Gloucester Falls to Chichester State Forest via The Mountaineer. You'll need the Barrington Tops and Chichester 1:25 000 maps. Plan a diversion to the abandoned Wangat village. This route could be extended to Newcastle, joining the Great North. Looking northwards it could easily extend itself to New England National Park, hence, an extraordinary link in the proposed Continental track spanning the Australian continent to its northern and southern extremities.

The Future

In the early 80s a major push for the conservation of the Barrington Tops rainforests led to government investigation. The resulting report led to park extensions, increasing its size from 16 000 ha. to over 39 000 ha. In the process three wilderness areas have been proposed: the upper Wangat River Valley or Chichester wilderness, the Boonabillla Creek region in the Park's south-west, and the Devil's Hole wilderness, east of Polblue. Larger, relatively undisturbed areas were designated as Natural Areas. These are mostly on the plateau itself.

What will happen now that recreational areas are more available, inexpensive, easily accessible and subject to future population pressures? What will happen too, if Australian cultural patterns tilt from a coastal, or beach, culture to a mountain-centred one? What pressures might be placed on areas such as Barrington Tops, the World Heritage Area closest to Sydney, and already a regular attraction for Newcastle and the Hunter Valley's 600 000 people?

It is not as far-fetched as many would believe: think of the increasing awareness of harmful effects of the sun's rays, the crowding of coastal areas, even global warming. Remember too the earlier heydays of the Blue Mountains, once the state's premier holiday centre. How would the authorities cope with a sudden influx?

These are questions that need to be ever present in the hearts and minds of all of us. For now there is an extremely good range of walking tracks. Elements of European and Aboriginal heritage coexist with a truly grand range of scenic and natural attractions.

In the future I still want to continue enjoy those frosty nights on the Tops, those treks through antarctic beech forest and sub alpine streams; I want to relax on the lower sites, enjoying the fireplace, rainforest fauna and sounds of mountain rivers. I only hope our children are so privileged.

NSW National Parks and Wildlife Service have produced a number of informative brochures on the park's features. These are available through the NPWS's Raymond Terrace office.

Contact:
The National Parks and Wildlife Service
Hunter Region
P.O. Box 270
Raymond Terrace 2324
Telephone: (049) 87 3108

It should also be noted that the Plan of Management for the Park may change the track system in a number of places. Check with the NPWS.

Footnotes

1 Barrington Tops NP Draft Plan of Management, 1989, p.14.
2 Just for fun, look at a map of the Hunter Valley and trace the source and direction of the Hunter River.
3 Enright, W. 1933. 'Further notes on the Worimi.' Mankind. 1(7):161-2. Mentioned in Byrne, Denis. The Aboriginal and Archaeological Significance of NSW Rainforests. Forestry and Heritage Commissions joint pub., 1987, p.23.
4 Letter no.14654, cited by Bryne,1987.
5 Read Les Murrays 'In a Working Forest', *Gone Bush*, Bantam Books, 1990.
6 Byrne, D., 1987, p.23.
7 Byrne, D., 1987, p.27.
8 Byrne, D., 1987, p.28.
9 See Barrington Tops NP Draft Plan of Management, 1989, pp.227.
10 This walk is based on the walk described in the NPWS brochure 'Rocky Crossing'.
11 I am indebted to a NPWS leaflet on this subject.

Considering Deep Pass

The **I was here** signs are plentiful; in the overhangs, on the walls and cliffs. Only they are not the work of vandals, but of past generations of Aborigines—multiple hand paintings found on sandstone walls. They're faint, but marvellous. This is Deep Pass, in the south-west corner of Wollemi National Park about 125 km south-west of Sydney.

Vehicles can get within 1.5 km of the Pass (see access map). By turning off the Bell to Lithgow road from Newnes Junction it is a 25 kilometre drive on rough forestry road to the turnoff. After 7 kilometres is Newnes Siding, the major siding of the old Newnes railway line. Although it is easily missed, if you stop and look into the bush you may notice the huge sweep of abandoned line where the trains would turn.

Later the forest road is followed through a pine plantation. The turnoff to the Pass comes where the pine forest has been cleared. Even then it is easy to miss, so a 1: 25 000 map is recommended.

After about five kilometres, park in a small clearing and then walk along an old access track, down a steep descent to a low saddle. Northward, through a fern glade and woodland, cliffs on either side, a 15-minute walk brings us to a grassy clearing. From here several gullies radiate outwards, each with their own attractions. To the south is a minor track to the Bungleboori wilderness. Above are cascading sandstone mountains leading into wilderness country. Head north to Deep Pass proper.

Walking here is easy. The tracks are short and well-defined and the surrounding bushland is pleasant and lightly wooded. A quick look around the sandstone walls will easily indicate where the hand paintings are likely to be. It's lots of fun seeking them out, and help can be gained from the maps for this chapter. In such surroundings the bush seems benevolent and welcoming.

But there should be limits! On my first visit I was surprised to see three 4WD vehicles parked in the central area of Deep Pass, a clearing reminiscent of a Victorian picnic ground. The vehicles were definitely transgressing, as signs near the parking area clearly indicate.

Vehicles using old access tracks typically intensify erosion. Also, they tend to introduce weeds by seeds carried in their tread. The machines are noisy and disturb the area's serenity. The passengers bring larger supplies of food and packaged goods, and they are less likely to take their rubbish out again. I asked myself what were these vehicles doing here?

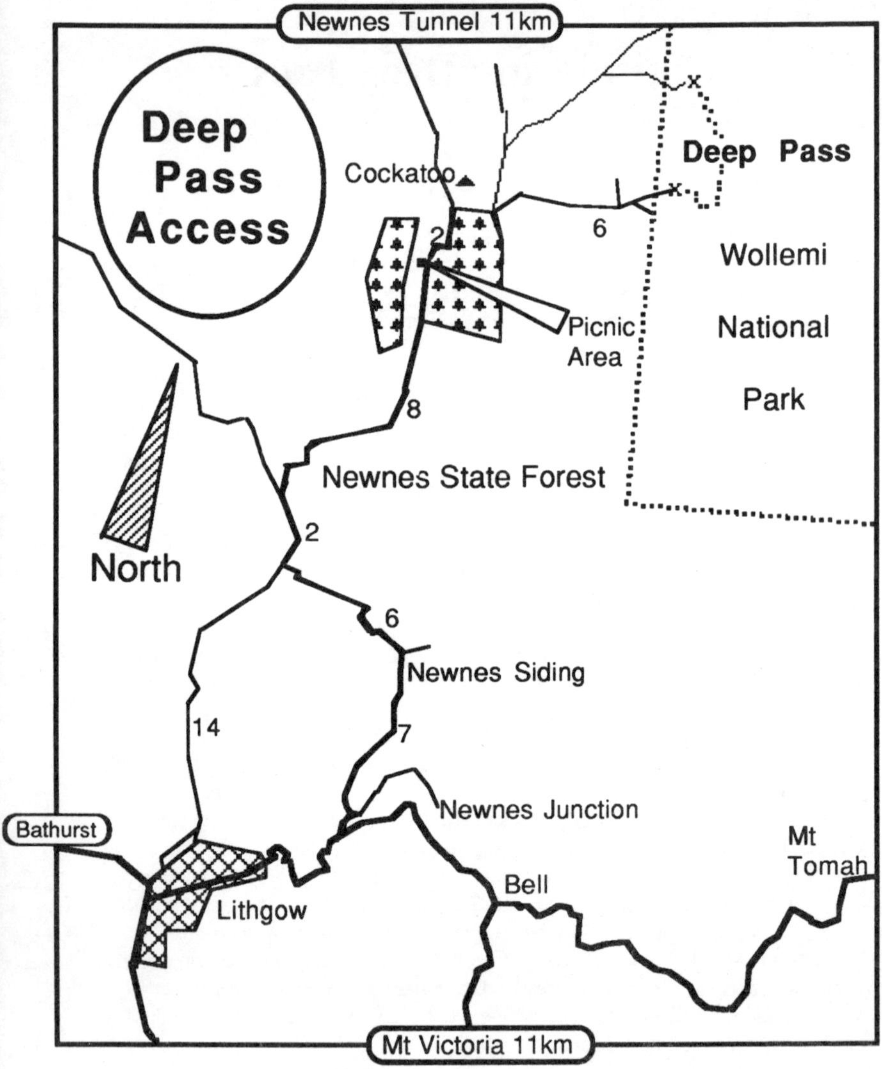
Newnes Tunnel 11km
Deep Pass Access
Cockatoo
Deep Pass
2
6
Wollemi
National
Park
Picnic
Area
8
Newnes State Forest
2
North
6
Newnes Siding
14
7
Newnes Junction
Bathurst
Mt
Tomah
Bell
Lithgow
Mt Victoria 11km

I went to question the owners, despite their unwelcoming air, opening with: 'how did you get down here?'—an irresistible invitation for two lads: 'It wasn't easy—chuckle chuckle—never thought we'd make it'—but the others' stony silence made them choke on their sentence. Social interaction ground to a halt, and we departed. There was no point in pursuing people who already knew they were guilty.

After a short stroll upstream we returned to find that they'd departed. Had the message got through, or were they just getting nervous? Either way the result was not satisfactory; these small acts of vandalism would continue tomorrow and the next. I wanted to phone up NPWS authorities and ask when would they introduce proper locked gates? Where is the management?, I might ask—to which they would no doubt reply: where is the money to manage?

In Deep Pass I felt a protective impulse. It is part of a national park and should not be subjected to such assaults. The incident set me thinking about both Deep Pass and its management.

But what is the heritage value of Deep Pass? Aboriginal habitation is apparently long. The nearest sites have at least three groups of hand paintings. A much shorter residence by Europeans has left the foundations of a homestead, the clearing itself and the remnants of a road.

Later recreational users, including four wheel drivers, bushwalkers and picnickers, have left numerous fireplaces, refuse, additional short tracks, ropes and steel spikes.

The NPWS assumed management of the area in 1979 with the formation of Wollemi National Park. In its short management span it appears that few changes have been made: just a parking space above, park entry restrictions and a road block.

From the inventory of remnants, which are heritage items, and which are forms of vandalism? Which are cases for conservation, which for removal? Are the hand paintings heritage or vandalism, and would additional hand painting 'improve' the landscape? Are steel pegs and ropes set in rocks vandalism or recreational facilities? Are 4WD visitors just asserting their rights? What harm is a little litter if more people visit the sites?

Now some questions might appear obvious or silly, but in visiting Deep Pass I've been forced to reconsider concepts like conservation, vandalism and management in order to discover what values and ideas make one thing heritage, another, vandalism. The two can be uncomfortably close, and our ability to rationalise is dangerous.

Take the hand paintings. Any addition to Aboriginal artworks would be an obvious act of vandalism. They despoil, are an act of fraud, and they decrease the value of the authentic works. Such an act would be arrogant, and a denial of the past. More wilful acts such as defacing or obliterating paintings can be seen as signs of resentment of the interest shown in Aboriginal culture today.

What about littering? Tins, bottles, foil and paper are commonly left behind

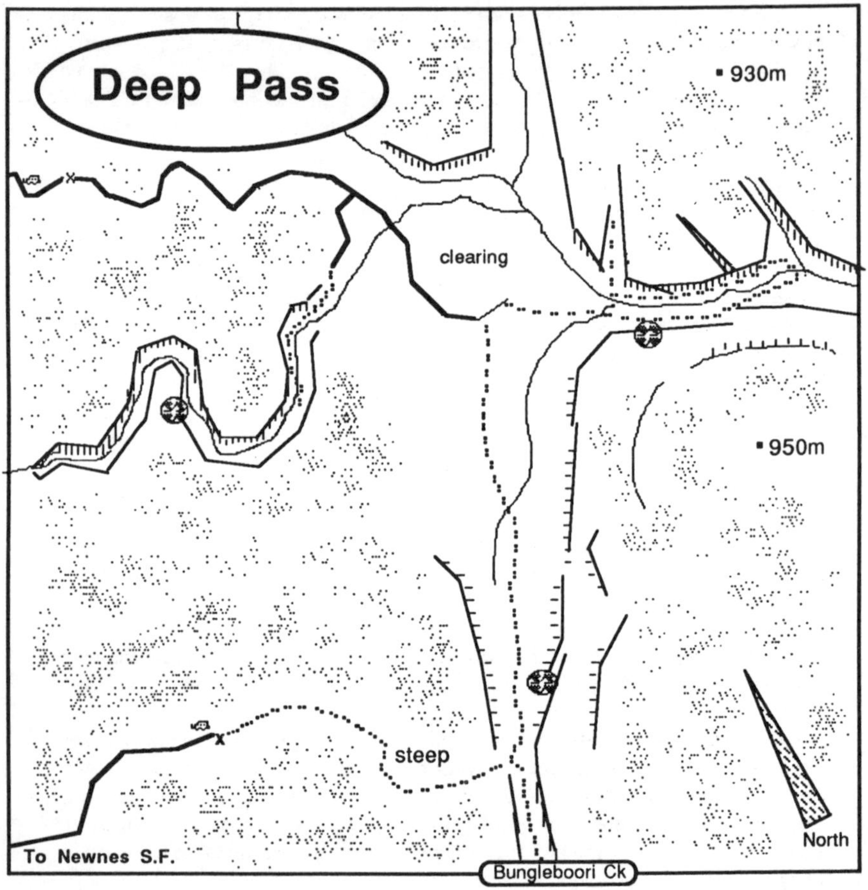
Deep Pass
930m
clearing
950m
steep
North
To Newnes S.F.
Bungleboori Ck

by visitors. Deep Pass certainly has a minor litter problem. Food is a particular problem, causing animals to become dependent on visitors' scraps, and also creating a bigger mess by rummaging.

The hand paintings of Deep Pass are heritage items of great value. They are found in three places that I know of: in an overhang, on a sheer wall, and in a relatively inaccessible chasm; all no more than few hundred metres apart.

Do the paintings indicate the place's importance, its degree of habitation or its frequent usage as a trading crossroad? At the very least they are assurance that Aborigines did indeed occupy the Pass. As evidence of the Aborigines' long habitation, even to the untutored the paintings suggest the presence of a site of rich archaeological significance, much of it buried all around the valley floor.

About 150 years ago, European settlers appeared. Are the landowner's changes also heritage items? Take, for example, the clearing. Once a cow pasture and site for a hut it had a destructive impact on the landscape. Might it be called historical vandalism? Settlers have arrived, it could be argued, cleared the gully of the original vegetation, made a road, built a hut and grazed cattle. Clearly vandalism, one may cry; just 'settling the country' says another.

Conservation (in the historical sense of the word) is the considered management of the past: what relics we have we can either pull down or preserve—or commemorate with a monument. We act to see that the past is remembered consistent with our perception of it. So it could be argued that the old hut and the clearing are worth preserving as a reminder of the small, subsistence landholdings found in remote regions.

But by what measure do we call this place 'historic'? If it is a relic, is it sufficiently important to warrant survival and maintenance?

Whether the clearing is an historic site or not, it does have value as a space for present and future recreational use. As well it could benefit visitors as an aid to the imagination. Any passing examination of the hut's foundations, for example, quickly acquaints us the settler's tiny living quarters; the cleared area is a reminder of the threat of fire to life and limb; the remoteness of the location an indication of a lonely existence, far from 'market' and from urban comforts. The clearing might also have hindered attack from Aborigines, or even cattle duffers.

Bushwalkers can't count themselves as innocents amongst sinners. Within the gorge are spikes and ropes used to climb up small cascades or through narrow gaps and deep pools. Without them access upstream is either blocked or accessible only to the more adventurous. Should they be preserved for current use, removed to restrict access or upgraded for greater recreational access? Despite the fact that they are aesthetically and environmentally fairly inoffensive, the question needs to be asked, if only to identify the shifting grounds of what constitutes vandalism. For the present the spikes provide valuable access (for some) to the hand paintings and the chasm. However authorities might rightly change their judgement should continued usage caused serious erosion or damage to hand stencils.

The Hand Paintings

Understanding history involves using the imagination. Try asking yourself: 'What was it like for the earliest occupants of Deep Pass?'; 'What were the cultural practices of the Aborigines?' or 'Do the hand paintings indicate that the Pass had either a particular or incidental significance?' These are exciting, imaginative challenges.

The sites of Deep Pass offer different perspectives of the Aboriginal past. One site, found under an eroded sandstone ledge, would have been an excellent shelter on rainy days. It is easy to imagine lighting a fire, warming up, telling a story, having a laugh, discussing problems, and leaving a handprint as a common mark of occupation. At another site the hands are painted onto a large vertical cliff. Here the site resembles an open air gallery. Importantly, it is close to water.

The third site is the most remote, hidden away on a curved wall deep in the Pass' long chasm. Standing inside such an natural feature is awesome; and the hands seem to stake a claim on the experience itself.The paintings seem to say: 'This is a place to be experienced, a place where we felt secure and in awe, a place that impressed us, as we have made an impression on it'. The act suggests an element of honouring the place through the image. Perhaps it was given a name, or became associated with a myth or story. The chasm's aura is certainly mysterious and powerful; being narrow, winding and high walled, the deep and hollow sounds that reverberate about the listener are bound to impress.

It is well known that hand paintings—usually of the left hand—were repainted from time to time. The process involved blowing either powdered or liquid ochre from the mouth or from a sheet of bark. On reflection, it's an act reaffirming ancestral connections and expressing a communal identity.

Like many a person I am happy just to be present at a site, especially when it has taken effort to reach it. In the creek chasm, for example, a rope is needed to mount the side of a cascade. On slippery surfaces or deep pools you need a secure footing. Having arrived I'm not at all moved to make my own mark. Why?

Perhaps I feel that the mark has already been made for me by those previous occupants. Generations have come, experienced, appreciated, and given the place a token of their presence. The fact that each generation contributed to the preservation of the hand paintings, is another potent reminder of a largely mysterious past.

Another reason might be the tremendous presumptuousness of such an act. How could I 'belong' to an Aboriginal past? I don't, as much as I respect and honour it.

Deep Pass can also produce a genuine awe of the natural world. Whether it is river or mountain chasm, the lower creek's rainforest environs or the lofty perches above the gorge, the contrasting intimacy and grandeur of Deep Pass are twin rewards.

To maintain that natural awe, access should be limited to walkers only. No vehicle access should be allowed; it is already degrading the flat, and further use risks vandalism and degradation. The track into the Pass is already heavily eroded, and growing worse. The noise and aggression of the engine destroys the rewards of solitude enjoyed by walkers. Vehicles turn the place into a parking lot.

The definition of a national park (quoted on page 9) adds another dimension: one of the functions of a national park is to cater for public recreation.

The forces acting on Deep Pass continue to press on it. Once far from population centres, modern transportation has brought it closer. Sydney is now less than three hours drive away. NPWS budgets are tight and funds needed for the Park are not available. Wollemi National Park and Deep Pass are increasingly vulnerable.

While recently introduced locked gates are sufficient to restrict 4WD vehicles, trail bikes remain unimpeded. As a result, wear and tear on the walking track is noticeable. When all is said and done, national parks require vigorous and well funded management.

The National Parks and Wildlife Service has been vigorously attacked by government, but not by government alone. Notions of 'user pays', admirable in many cases, may be inappropriate in others. Often it is an administrative nightmare; sometimes it is an assault on the enjoyment of life itself. Such rationalist solutions are reaching the point where they reduce values to arithmetic measure, to cold dollars and cents. There is room yet for further vandalism in Deep Pass, but who will be responsible? The writing is on the wall.

The National Parks and Wildlife Code

The preservation and protection of our natural areas depends on the cooperation of all who visit and enjoy our national parks and nature reserves. Here are a few simple rules that everyone is asked to observe:

• Wildfire can destroy lives and property, so be careful, especially during the bush fire danger periods. Use only safe fireplaces and do not light fires during total fire ban periods.

• Keep the areas you use tidy—place rubbish in the bins where provided or take it away with you.

• Leave your pets at home—they can disturb and kill native animals and are often a nuisance to the other visitors.

• Leave firearms at home.

• Do not disturb plants, animals and rocks. Rocks are important shelter for some animals and plants.

• Drive carefully and keep to roads and car parks provided.

• Please observe all signs. They are provided for your guidance and to assist you to enjoy the areas you visit.

Further Reading

General

Australian Mythologica; Sites/Sights/Cites. A Third Degree Publication, 1986.
A Field Guide to Aboriginal Rock Engravings. Stanbury & Clegg. OUP, 1990.
National Parks of NSW. Gregories, 1984.
The Macquarie Book of Events. 1984.
The Economic Development of Australia. A.G.L. Shaw. Longman, 1970.
Native Plants of the Sydney Region. Baker, Corringham and Dark. Three Sisters, 1986.
Wild Foods of Australia. A.B. and J.W. Cribb. Fontana, 1974.
Inventing Australia. Richard White. Allen and Unwin, 1981.
Spoils and Spoilers, Geoffrey Bolton. Allen and Unwin, 1981.
The Songlines. Bruce Chadwin. Penguin, 1988.

Six Foot Track

From Katoomba to Jenolan Caves. Jim Smith. Second Back Row Press, 1984.
'Jenolan Caves: Special Management Needs'. Chris Chaffe, pp.27-8. *National Park Journal*. Dec.1988.
Landlopers. John Le Gay Brereton, 1899.
Knocking Around. John Le Gay Brereton, 1930.
'The Bridle Track to Jenolan'. Dowdy. *Sydney Mail*, 6/3/1891.
'New Route from Katoomba to the Fish River Caves'. Irlswith, *Sydney Mail*, 12/7/1884.
'A Walking Expedition', H. Tompkins, *Sydney Mail*, 18/12/1912.
The Heyday of Natural History. Lynn Barber. Doubleday, 1980.
Social Sketches of Australia 1888-1975. H. McQueen. Penguin, 1978.

The Corn Trail

'The Historic Corn Trail'. Brochure. Historic Tracks and Research Group, with Forestry Commission support.
'The Corn Trail', Dennis Moore. pp.39-42, *Heritage Australia*. Date Unknown.
The Vegetation and Flora of the Historic 'Corn Trail', State Forest. Phillip Craven. Unpublished report, 1988.

Murramarang National Park

'Murramarang—National Park or Public Domain?'. Pat Thompson. pp.29-30, *National Parks Journal*, December,1988.

The Passage, Vance Palmer. Robertson & Mullins, 1944.
Various NPWS leaflets on Murramarang.

Budawang Range

Pigeon House and Beyond. The Budawang Committee. 1987.
Burnam Burnam's Aboriginal Australia. Angus & Robertson. 1988.
Bushwalking in the Budawangs. Ron Doughton. Envirobook, 1989.
The Man from the Misty Mountains. James Sturgiss. The Budawang Committee, 1986

Barrington Tops

The Aboriginal and Archaeological Significance of the NSW Rainforests. Denis Byrne. Forestry Commission of NSW and Australian Heritage Commission. 1987.
Barrington Tops National Park: Draft Plan of Management. NPWS (NSW),1989.
Various NPWS leaflets for Barrington Tops National Parks.
Gone Bush. Readings. R. McDonald (ed). Bantam Books, 1991.
National Parks of Northern NSW. NSW National Parks Association. 1991.

Index